THE
EVERYTHING®
Mother
of the
Bride
Book

4TH EDITION

The ultimate wedding planning guide for Mom!

Katie Martin

adamsmedia
Avon, Massachusetts

An Everything® Series Book.
Everything® and everything.com® are registered trademarks of F+W Media, Inc.

Published by
Adams Media, a division of F+W Media, Inc.
57 Littlefield Street, Avon, MA 02322. U.S.A.
www.adamsmedia.com

ISBN 10: 1-4405-8820-1
ISBN 13: 978-1-4405-8820-4
eISBN 10: 1-4405-8821-X
eISBN 13: 978-1-4405-8821-1

Printed in the United States of America.

10   9   8   7   6   5   4   3   2   1

Library of Congress Cataloging-in-Publication Data
Martin, Katie.
    The everything mother of the bride book / Katie Martin. -- Fourth edition.
        pages cm. -- (An Everything series book)
    Includes index.
    ISBN 978-1-4405-8820-4 (pb) -- ISBN 1-4405-8820-1 (pb) -- ISBN 978-1-4405-
8821-1 (ebook) -- ISBN 1-4405-8821-X (ebook)
    1. Wedding etiquette. 2. Weddings--Planning. I. Title.
    BJ2051.H34 2015
    395.2'2--dc23

                                    2015000811

This publication is designed to provide accurate and authoritative information
with regard to the subject matter covered. It is sold with the understanding that
the publisher is not engaged in rendering legal, accounting, or other professional
advice. If legal advice or other expert assistance is required, the services of a com-
petent professional person should be sought.
    —From a *Declaration of Principles* jointly adopted by a Committee of the
American Bar Association and a Committee of Publishers and Associations

Many of the designations used by manufacturers and sellers to distinguish their
products are claimed as trademarks. Where those designations appear in this
book and F+W Media, Inc. was aware of a trademark claim, the designations have
been printed with initial capital letters.

Cover images © Teerawut Masawat/123RF.

This book is available at quantity discounts for bulk purchases.
For information, please call 1-800-289-0963.

THE

EVERYTHING

MOTHER OF THE BRIDE BOOK

4th Edition

Dear Reader,

After being in the wedding industry for over sixteen years, I still love every conversation I have with moms of brides-to-be who have recently become engaged. The best part of the wedding day is seeing a mother hold back her tears as she watches her baby girl head down the aisle.

Yes, I love weddings and have yet to become jaded. That's because every wedding introduces me to new and interesting ideas. When it comes to planning weddings, one of my greatest resources is you—the mother, stepmother, grandmother, or godmother. You have watched your little girl mature, find her own style, and refine her tastes. You know what makes her tick and what ticks her off. The mother-daughter wedding planning experience can be fraught with emotions, but thankfully, your daughter has you to help her.

My own wedding was something my mom and I loved doing together. She leaned on my experience, and I leaned on her for guidance and wisdom with the new extended family that I was marrying into. I was able to see my mom's part in the wedding much more clearly after watching so many MOBs over the years. It was a blessing for me to watch my mom thoroughly enjoy my wedding day!

It is my hope that by picking up this book, you will start the wedding planning process with the tools you need to make it one you and your daughter will savor and remember with a smile. My mom and I wish you all the joy that we experienced and more!

Katie Martin

OCT - - 2016

The EVERYTHING Series

These handy, accessible books give you all you need to tackle a difficult project, gain a new hobby, or even brush up on something you learned back in school but have since forgotten. You can read from cover to cover or just pick out information from our four useful boxes.

 Alerts: Urgent warnings

 Essentials: Quick handy tips

 Facts: Important snippets of information

 Questions: Answers to common questions

When you're done reading, you can finally say you know **EVERYTHING**®!

PUBLISHER Karen Cooper

MANAGING EDITOR, EVERYTHING® SERIES Lisa Laing

COPY CHIEF Casey Ebert

ASSISTANT PRODUCTION EDITOR Alex Guarco

ACQUISITIONS EDITOR Hillary Thompson

DEVELOPMENT EDITOR Eileen Mullan

EVERYTHING® SERIES COVER DESIGNER Erin Alexander

Visit the entire Everything® series at *www.everything.com*

Dedication

Para mi hija, Elena, y mi "hija," Wendy, y su hija, Gema. ¡Les amo mucho! For my son. I promise to be the best mother of the groom (one day . . . like when you are 30)! *Para mi Miguel ¡Te amo siempre!*

Acknowledgments

Thank you, Alison De Wit, for reminding me that grammar is always of utmost importance. Thanks (and a huge hug) to Stefanie Manns for always saving me in the editing department. Thanks again to Grace and Hillary—I am forever grateful for the opportunities you have given me!

THE TOP TEN THINGS THE MOB
SHOULD BE READY TO SAY

1. It's not my wedding. It's yours, honey!

2. Of course you can have a dessert bar instead of a wedding cake.

3. No problem, the check is on the way.

4. Need my credit card number?

5. How cute that you picked blue shoes for your "something blue"!

6. Your bridesmaids can spend the night.

7. Your dad loves the outfit you picked out for him.

8. Whatever color you like, sweetheart.

9. Sure, I can pick up the stamps.

10. Instagram it!

Contents

Introduction 11

1. The Engagement **15**
Start Spreading the News! 16
Careful Sharing with Social Media 19
Communication with the Bride 21
Whose Wedding Is It? 23
Engagement Party 27
Getting Organized 30

2. Meeting His Family **33**
Your New Son-in-Law 34
Meeting His Family 36
The Mother of the Groom 39
Planning with His Family 42
Rehearsal Dinner Etiquette 44
Family Traditions 45

3. Money Matters **52**
Bride's Family: Traditional Expenses 53
The Groom's Family 55
Budget for Today's Weddings 56
Finding the Money 61
Destination Wedding Expenses 64
Post-Wedding Expenses 69
Gratuity Basics 71

4. Your Responsibilities **74**
Traditional MOB Responsibilities 75

What's Expected of You and When. 77
How to Avoid the *Pushy MOB* Label 80
Keeping Dad in the Loop 81
Above and Beyond. 83
Wedding Planners and Family Help 87
Nontraditional Wedding Basics 92

5. Wedding Planning 411 . . . . **95**
Your Timeline and Plan. 96
Eco-Friendly Options. 98
Ceremony and Reception Basics 101
Photography and Videography. 107
Entertainment. 110
Flowers and Décor 113
Transportation. 115
Accommodations 116
Details 118

6. The Savvy Social Media MOB. **120**
Using Social Media Gracefully. 121
Guest Considerations. 123
Wedding, Health, and Fashion Blogs. 124
Pinterest 130
Facebook. 132
Instagram 134
Twitter 135
Tumblr 136
Google+ 137
Wedding Apps for the Big Day. 138
"Unplugged" Weddings. 140

7. Let the (Other) Parties Begin! **141**
Party-Planning Basics 142
Stifle Those Comments, Mom 145
Bridal Shower 148
Bridesmaids' Luncheon 154
Bachelorette Party 157
Welcome Reception and Rehearsal 157
Post-Wedding Reception 158
Brunch 158
Speech Hints and Tips 159

8. Dressing the Part **160**
Simple Rules for Yourself 161
The Perfect Dress—Where Is It? 164
The Bride's Dress 170
Buyer Be *Very* Wary 174
MOB Beauty and Pampering 177

9. Delicate Situations **178**
Family Dynamics 179
An Ex-Family Reunion 183
Step Right Up, Calling All Stepmothers! 186
Keeping the Peace 189
Special Roles 192
Second Weddings 193
Same-Sex Weddings 196

10. The Guest List **201**
One for You, and One for Me 202
Who's In, Who's Out 202
The Second Wedding 206
The B List 208

Selecting the Invitations. 210
Putting It All Together 213

11. Where and How to Save Money 218
The Ground Rules. 219
Flower Power 222
The Dresses. 227
The Bar Tab 231
The Invitations. 235
Going Green 236
Other Ways to Save 237

12. Wedding-Day Overview 241
Be Prepared 242
Pre-Wedding Preparations 243
Flowers? Check! 246
Off to the Ceremony!. 249
The Interim 252
The Reception. 254
"Hostess with the Mostest" 260
Toasting Basics 261

13. The Best Mother-in-Law Ever 262
Thank-You Notes. 263
The Newlyweds' Attitude. 266
Last but Not Least 270

Appendix A: Planning Timeline 272

Appendix B: What Are You Saying?
Invitation Wording. 276

Index. 284

Introduction

Your daughter has finally reached you on your cell phone to proclaim the news, "I'm engaged!" You are thrilled and eager to broadcast the engagement to your husband, family, friends, and coworkers. Within the next few hours, you will have already planned out the entire wedding with a reception at your beach home. Wait! This is your daughter's wedding, not yours. She really loves winter, hates wearing bathing suits, and she did mention the historical mansion near her favorite park downtown during her phone call. Reality sets in and you ask yourself: now what? Since weddings have changed significantly over the years, this eternal question is not quickly or easily answered.

In the past, it was the mother of the bride's duty to take care of every detail of the wedding. She would make almost all of the decisions, and the bride simply needed to pick out her dress and smile as she floated down the aisle. Oh, how the times have changed! Extended and divorced families (along with the rising average age of a bride) have completely changed a mother's role in planning her daughter's wedding. Real weddings are showcased on TV, in newspapers, online, and in pretty much all media outlets. Brides are now the focal point of the wedding planning process. Brides also have a lot more buying power and are willing to pay for things that you might think are ridiculous.

This does not mean you will be banished from making decisions or offering opinions and advice; it simply means you'll need to find different ways to communicate with your daughter.

Some brides take immense pleasure in planning their own wedding—they may want it to reflect their sense of style and personality. On the other hand, many brides would be lost without their mothers' guidance during the planning process. Perhaps you have entertained a lot, and she will be more than happy to let you make most of the plans. Just look at the two most important factors of the planning process: your relationship with your daughter, and who is holding the purse strings. Remember, whether you do most of the work or only a part, it will help if you are prepared and knowledgeable.

The budget and the size of the wedding should always be the first two items discussed, since one depends on the other. There are traditional expenses for your family and her fiancé's family. However, tradition may go out the window depending on the type of wedding your daughter and her fiancé want to have. They may want to pay for most of the items for the wedding or divide the cost with you. His parents may want to break tradition to contribute a significant amount to finance their son's wedding, or the opposite might be true. You may not be in a position to help much monetarily but can contribute in other ways.

After the budget is confirmed, you and the bride need to divide and conquer! You will spend countless hours discussing venues, colors, dresses, flowers, photography, cuisine, entertainment, and hundreds of other decisions. The time has come to do the research, interview the vendors, reconnect with family and friends, and prepare yourself and the bride for the wedding day. Take it one step at a time (and one vendor at a time), and you will enjoy the process more and be delighted with the results on the wedding day. The role of mother of the bride is a hectic but rewarding one, so savor and remember it every step of the way. All of the planning and stress will be worth it when you see your daughter walk down the aisle with her new spouse. Congratulations!

CHAPTER 1

The Engagement

A mother knows when her daughter's relationship with a certain man is turning serious. There will be talk of this man's absolute perfection, a mention or two of his plans for the future, and eventually the M word (that would be *marriage*) starts slipping into conversation. Finally seeing that ring on her finger will be an exciting moment, even if you knew it was coming. Meanwhile, you are automatically appointed mother of the bride. What does this mean to you . . . and to everyone else?

Start Spreading the News!

Before your daughter and her fiancé start shouting from the rooftops, spreading their engagement news far and wide, who should be told first? (Or, actually, second—after you?) It's important that the people closest to them hear about their upcoming wedding before the rest of the world does. This might mean that you have to sit on this information until both families have seen the ring with their own eyes.

 Essential

Express yourself when your daughter announces her big news to you, even if you're stone-faced about almost everything in life. Be flattered that she came to you. This is an important gesture for your daughter.

Telling the Rest of the Gang

Who's next? Anyone with a vested interest in this wedding should not hear about it on social media. The couple should be the ones to announce the engagement to his parents. You are not permitted to jump the gun and call your daughter's future in-laws before they even know that they're about to become her in-laws.

Once the VIPs have been told about the engagement, the rest of the world is ready to hear about it. Make some phone calls to the relatives, or send out a slew of e-mails. You don't need to send out formal announcements, but you may if you are moved to do so.

Making the Announcement

If they plan to submit a picture and formal announcement to the local paper, your daughter and her fiancé may want to make an appointment with a photographer to have a formal engagement portrait done. Depending on the length of the engagement, they may have some time on their hands before taking care of this, or they could find themselves rushing to a photographer immediately.

 **Question**

When is the appropriate time to make an announcement in the newspaper?

The engagement announcement (with or without picture) should really appear no sooner than six months prior to the wedding date—three to four months before the big day is ideal. Check your local newspaper (or paper of choice) for its particular deadline and recommendations, which are usually published on the website.

What Should the Announcement Say?

The announcement will include the couple's information (schooling, occupations, where they're living now, where they will live after the ceremony), along with their parents' names. Most newspapers simply have forms for the bride and groom to fill out. If her fiancé's family lives elsewhere, make sure they receive a copy of the engagement photo so that they can put an announcement in their own local newspaper.

Listing (All) the Parents

If both sets of biological parents happen to be still married, writing the announcement is a piece of cake. Simply include where each set of parents lives, and it's done. If one or both sets of parents are divorced, the only effect it has on the announcement is that it will be longer—in order to include all of the parents' names.

For example, if both sets of parents are divorced, and every parent has remarried, the section of the announcement pertaining to them would read: "The bride is the daughter of Mr. and Mrs. Edward Smith of York, Maine, and Mr. and Mrs. Thomas Dolittle of Bakersfield, California. The groom is the son of Mr. and Mrs. Allen Fox of Chicago, Illinois, and Mr. and Mrs. Gregory Brown of Boston, Massachusetts."

 Fact

In the case of naming a divorced single mother on either side of the wedding, use the name she prefers. She may still prefer to be called Mrs. So-and-So (her former husband's first and last name), or she may simply go by her first and last name, without a "Mrs." or "Ms."

An example of an announcement where one or more parents have remained single would read:

"The bride is the daughter of Ms. Valerie Turner of York, Maine, and Mr. and Mrs. Thomas Dolittle of Bakersfield, California. The groom is the son of Mr. and

Mrs. Allen Fox of Chicago, Illinois, and Mr. Gregory Brown of Boston, Massachusetts."

Careful Sharing with Social Media

Since the onslaught of social media, brides (and their moms) have loved the idea of sharing every single detail of their wedding planning. However, privacy issues and problems have arisen in the media in general due to social media. There is such a thing as "oversharing" and being a "serial Instagrammer." Heed some warnings when it comes to sharing your daughter's wedding plans and the wedding day.

Have a Social Media Plan

One of the biggest mistakes that modern parents make is sharing something that the couple wanted to remain a secret for the wedding day. Have a plan with your daughter as to what you can and can't share. Many couples want to keep everything a secret, and some couldn't care less. You really have to communicate with them before you post something to any social media platform.

Social Media–Free Weddings

Many couples have made a conscious choice to keep everything about their wedding offline. Some of this is due to personal circumstances, and some people are just very private. Everything that is posted online, stays online . . . forever! For example, there might be legal, work, or privacy reasons due to a previous marriage and children being involved. Ex-spouses continue to be a reality for the modern-day couple, and some are worse than others. Keeping the wedding safe and private is not a bad thing. It just means it is not online. Try not to argue against this, as weddings have always been private affairs. Not sharing the details online will keep the entire world out of your daughter's wedding day!

 **Essential**

If your daughter is all about having a social media–free wedding, make sure her wishes are made abundantly clear to guests. You can have the couple post this on their password-protected wedding website. You can also display signage at the ceremony, along with a reminder printed in the program. Ask the officiant to make an announcement about it as well at the beginning of the ceremony.

Not Going Viral

The point of carefully sharing photos during the wedding planning process (and not necessarily going viral) is to share only glimpses of things. For example, if you have ordered a five-tier wedding cake with each tier having a different design (and five amazing, different flavors), place a photo of only the piece of cake that you tried at the tasting. This sample looks nothing like what the cake will look like the day of the wedding, so you aren't giving any real details away. However, you can tag where you are (so they know you are at one of the best wedding cake designers in town) and share how excited you are about what you have tasted. But showing the sketch and the color details and naming every single cake flavor for the cake on Instagram and Facebook should not be done. You don't need your daughter's wedding day going viral.

Communication with the Bride

No matter how many events you have pulled off in your life, there is nothing like planning a wedding with your daughter. If you read any part of this book, these next few paragraphs are key to keeping you and your daughter sane. As in any relationship, communication is the key!

Phone, E-Mail, and Chat

If you and your daughter are planning the wedding together, you must decide how you will communicate with each other. Details and decisions will be crucial, and communicating these items will help avoid extra work. If you don't have an e-mail address, create one. If you don't get on the Internet that much, start! If you don't have a smartphone, get one! Brides today are doing most of their planning and information gathering online and on their smartphones. You can talk on the phone, but be ready for a barrage of e-mails detailing photos and website addresses for the dress, shoes, flowers, linens, etc., to be the backbone of the conversations you are having on the phone. In addition to phone and e-mail discussions, you may want to consider online chats and web conferencing if you and your daughter live far apart from each other.

Free online chat services are available, and all you need is a computer with a built-in webcam or an external webcam that you plug into your computer.

However, you will make your life much easier if you get a smartphone that allows you to talk face-to-face with a camera built into the phone. This way, when your daughter is at the florist downtown and you are picking up the bridesmaids' dresses at the seamstress, she can simply show you what the flowers look like while talking it through with you at the same time.

Using Social Media for Communicating

While it may be true that your daughter does not want just anyone to know all the details of her wedding day on social media, there is a way to share with close friends and family. You can make your Instagram account open to the public but password-protected, so that only certain people can see the Instagram photos. This way, you, the bride, and her bridesmaids can all like or make comments on fun details of the wedding throughout the whole process without letting the world know about it! You can also create a private Facebook page. The list goes on and on with all the social media apps that are available for sharing photos online. You can learn more about all the major forms of social media later on in Chapter 6!

Keep on the Subject

No matter how wonderful your relationship is with your daughter, try to keep wedding conversations about the wedding. It is easy to bring in emotional sidebars about uncomfortable situations, since weddings tend to bring out both the emotional best and worst in people. Miscommunication about what the bride wants and what you want can easily be avoided if you simply carve out a specific time to talk about the wedding on a weekly basis. Whatever is not discussed during these specific times can be fleshed out in e-mail! Don't let the wedding get in the way of regular mother-daughter conversations.

Whose Wedding Is It?

It's so exciting to think about planning the wedding of your—err, your daughter's—dreams, isn't it? Some moms are surprised to find themselves at complete odds with their girls when it comes to even the most basic planning steps. Are you thinking of a white-tie affair with 300 guests, while your daughter is talking about a wedding in the woods with only immediate family in attendance? You must show her the error of her ways, mustn't you?

Pull Back

If the bride is planning to pay for most of this wedding herself, you really can't expect her to change her plans in favor of your wildly different ideas. This is her wedding, after all, especially in the case of the bride and groom who are doing all the legwork and footing the bill. They're in charge. Does this mean you can't offer any helpful advice? As long as you can remain helpful (and do not become a bully), you can certainly help out when and where the bride requests it of you. Otherwise, silence is golden.

On the other hand, if you (and/or your husband or the bride's dad—whatever the case may be) are paying for most of this wedding, you are entitled to some input. However, you should try to respect the bride's general wishes.

Remember, It's Her Party

This leads to a discussion on the wedding you wish you could have had—if only you and your family could have afforded it then. Now, you're rolling in money (or you have enough, at least, to make your daughter's wedding a lavish event), and darn it, this wedding is going to be everything you wanted, whether your daughter agrees or not. (She doesn't realize what she's turning down, and you know she'll be sorry if she misses out on having a huge wedding.) Hijacking her wedding to alleviate your own regrets is a bad idea; you had your turn to be the bride. Let your daughter have her turn now. If you do not concede to items that are important to your daughter, it will create tension and frustration for all.

 Alert

First things first: You and the bride need to touch base on major wedding issues before anyone signs contracts with vendors. These include the size of the wedding, how formal an affair she's picturing, and her preferred season. The answers to these questions give you a baseline to work from.

If she's left the planning completely in your hands, you're technically free to do whatever you want. Unless she specifically tells you otherwise, it would be in your best interest to double-check certain details with her. (Chicken or beef for dinner? Buffet stations or sit-down meal?) And once you have her opinions, don't disregard them, even if you disagree with them. This is a leading cause of daughters and mothers not speaking to each other during the bride's engagement period.

You *Aren't* Made of Money?

You may find yourself talking to a bride who has absolutely no concept of the value of a dollar and/or no idea about how much things cost. She may be the one making a guest list that seemingly includes a small nation, and you may be the one who has to break the news about the budget to her. She may retort with "It's my wedding! We have to do it my way!" Mom, you've got your work cut out for you.

 Essential

Yes, you want to give her the wedding of her dreams, but realistically, you can only do so much. It's not wise for you to go into massive debt just so your daughter can have the most opulent party your hometown has ever seen.

If you find yourself in this less-than-enviable position, break it to her gently—but firmly. Perhaps you can still pull off the wedding she wants if the two of you can agree on how to cut corners in some areas. (She wants 300 people at the reception? Fine. They won't be eating prime rib, and they may find themselves standing in a picnic grove instead of a hotel ballroom.)

Dealing with the bride who has delusions of grandeur is sometimes tough, but if the two of you can put your heads together and get creative, she may be able to have a wedding worthy of her dreams—and you'll be able to sleep, knowing that you still have some money left over.

This All Seems Very Familiar . . .

If you've already planned a wedding or two for your other daughters, your first instinct may be to plan the exact same affair for this bride-to-be. After all, what's good enough for her sisters is good enough for her. And besides, you can't very well show any favoritism between the girls, so you have to keep their weddings even.

That thought process is admirable; however, "even" doesn't always mean "identical." Chances are, the same members of your family who were at the previous wedding will be at this one, too. You're likely to hear mumbles along the lines of "Wow, they must really like this place," and "They must really like the fish here, because we had it at the other reception, too." You're spending an awful lot of money on this—is that really the reaction you want?

Even if your daughter is comfortable with the idea of duplicating her sister's wedding, avoid the urge to do so. Your girls aren't carbon copies of one another, and even if they're very much alike and have always wanted very similar weddings, your currently engaged daughter will have some ideas of her own.

Fact

Asking mothers of other recently married brides about their experiences is a great way to get ideas for your daughter's wedding. Magazines, websites, and blogs are all great resources for getting advice and ideas.

Engagement Party

Once you and your daughter have fleshed out some of the overall ideas for her wedding, the time will come to decide whether or not you will want to hold an engagement party. The options are endless, but try not to let the engagement party outshine the wedding with all the new excitement in the air!

The Etiquette of Engagement Parties

The bride's family has the option of throwing the first engagement party, according to traditional wedding etiquette. You are not in any way obligated to do so, and if you're planning on contributing significantly to the wedding itself, you may feel as though the responsibility of hosting this party should really fall on someone else's shoulders. Whatever position you find yourself in (hostess or guest), you'll need to know what to do, what to wear, and what you'll say when everyone raises their champagne flutes and looks to you.

The Basics

You've decided to follow tradition and toast your daughter and soon-to-be son-in-law. When? Where? How? It's best to plan the engagement party well in advance of other pre-wedding events so that it stands on its own for what it is—a happy celebration of the couple's decision to spend their lives together. If the bride and groom are having a long engagement (a year or longer), an engagement party would be appropriate six to eight months before the actual ceremony.

Different hosts have different ideas for engagement parties. Can you go all out and book the fanciest hotel in the city for this event? Sure. But might you also go to the other extreme and clean off the grill for an outdoor patio engagement party? Yes, as long as the bride and groom don't have a serious problem with an ultracasual affair. Keep in mind that the engagement party shouldn't outshine the wedding. If your daughter is planning a simple little ceremony, the engagement party should be scaled down to a similar level of informality.

Obviously, the location of the event and the time of day will play a large part in dictating the menu. Most engagement parties tend to swing toward cocktails and hors d'oeuvres, but you can certainly break that tradition if you have your heart set on a catered meal with all the accoutrements. (Chances are your guests won't complain if you want to spoil them a bit.) And no matter how formal the party gets, the couple shouldn't expect to open gifts at the end of the night—presents are not traditionally given at engagement parties.

The Guest List

The guest list for the engagement party causes some hostesses a lot of grief. It's best to stick with the old, standard rule: Anyone who is invited to a pre-wedding party must also be invited to the wedding. It's just in poor taste to invite a guest to celebrate an upcoming event and then exclude that guest from that very event.

 **Essential**

> Don't offend friends and/or relatives by inviting them to pre-wedding parties when they won't be invited to the wedding. If the bride and groom are hosting their own engagement party, you probably can't stop errant invitations. If *you're* the hostess, though, the guest list is largely your responsibility.

Put yourself in the position of these guests of convenience: Would you want to attend a party to honor people who weren't going to somehow squeeze you into the major festivities? You'd probably feel hurt when you learned that you weren't important enough to the engaged couple to make the final cut.

Be Their Guest

If someone else (the groom's family, the bride's friends, or the bride and groom themselves) decides to host the engagement party, what are you expected to do? You're expected to show up and to be good company. You're expected to lend a hand if and when it's needed, without crossing into controlling territory, which means you'll attend the party with an on-call attitude. You won't be involved in the planning, and you won't be responsible for the execution of the party, but because you are the MOB, you really should keep an eye out for any trouble spots. Is the host having trouble greeting guests and hanging their coats? Grab some hangers and help out. Are some of the guests looking for napkins and having no luck? Pop into the kitchen and grab a stack.

It's easy to fall into the trap of doing so much that the host actually gets offended—as though you're trying to take over a party that you're not sponsoring—so when in doubt, ask. Being helpful is a wonderful trait in an MOB, and few folks would refuse the assistance—but some will.

Getting Organized

Eventually, the novelty of telling everyone that your daughter is engaged will wear off, and you'll realize that you have an event to plan. If you've never put a wedding together before, you may be incredibly excited at the prospect of interviewing caterers and photographers, and, hopefully, your experience will be trouble-free. Unfortunately, that's not always the case. The two most important things that you can do are get organized and ask questions.

Enlisting Help
Don't try to do everything yourself. If your daughter isn't available to help out, enlist the help of your sister, a

friend, or your husband. Planning a wedding is a big job, and the more hands to help lighten your load, the better.

 Alert

When you enlist the help of others, you must always keep in mind what your daughter wants! Don't let people interject too many of their own opinions, and especially do not let your own taste and style get in the way of what the couple wants.

Timeline

Making a timeline will be the best thing you can do for yourself when organizing and planning for your daughter's wedding. Once the engaged couple has set the date, you can lay out a time frame that works best for you and your daughter to plan.

The Notebook

Your daughter, if she is the organized type, will start putting together a notebook of sorts, either electronically or in an actual notebook, to collect and organize her wedding details. If not, you should take charge and have a notebook. There has to be a centralized place where contracts, photos, and ideas are kept.

In a nutshell, keep all of your information together—in a file, a notebook, a drawer—where it's easily accessible. Don't leave brochures scattered all over your home, or you'll only add to your stress.

Wedding Professionals

Getting organized before meeting with a wedding professional is essential. Whether you are going to these meetings together or separately, get organized for each vendor. Have a list of questions for each type of wedding professional. Don't leave a meeting with a vendor until you're clear on every issue you wanted to address. These people get paid (at least in part) to answer potential customers' queries, and they want your business.

The Guest Lists

During the planning process you will have multiple guest lists. Invest in a spreadsheet program to help keep track of who is invited to which events (or make this part of your notebook). Remember, you will have various parties to attend and host. Be sure that you take note of the guest list for every party that you do not host. This is of utmost importance when it comes to the actual wedding guest list. Your daughter and her fiancé will need to help communicate these lists to you when you are not the actual host. This will also help spark conversation at all pre-wedding and post-wedding events.

Keeping everything organized will not only help you reduce the stress that most weddings induce but will also help you enjoy the process. Asking questions will alleviate awkward conversations with the bride, groom, family, and friends. It will also reduce buyer's remorse and help foster great relationships with all of your wedding professionals.

CHAPTER 2

Meeting His Family

*Y*our daughter is starting a new marriage with your soon-to-be son-in-law. Taking the time to get to know the groom and his family can make all the difference in the world, not only for the wedding planning process, but also for the years that come after.

Your New Son-in-Law

Because many young women are waiting until they're out of college and established in their careers—sometimes across the country from where you live—to settle down with the perfect guy, your daughter may come home already engaged to a man you've never laid eyes on (at least not in person). Of course, you trust her judgment, so you're willing to go on the assumption that he's a great guy. But how can you establish your own relationship with him? After all, the two of you are going to be in each other's lives forever, starting now, so you want to make sure that you get off to a good start.

Getting to Know You . . .

Now that you have met him, it's time to get to know him. Right away you will probably want to know everything about him, if your daughter has not already filled you in on the details. Take some time to sit down with him and ask important questions, including:

- What he does for a living
- His interests and hobbies
- His plans for the future (say, if he's in grad school, or if he's talking about a move out West)
- Whether he has a former wife and/or children (because they will hugely affect your daughter's life)

The first time you meet your daughter's future husband, you want to find acceptance while keeping your daughter's best interest at heart. Now is not the time to bring up major issues or provoke confrontation. If you have concerns about their financial and emotional future, tread lightly and start with talking to your daughter first.

 Alert

Go into your first conversation with this guy with an open mind, and promise yourself not to make any snap judgments. There is plenty of time for a full evaluation of him—just not during your initial meeting.

Easy Does It, Mom

So, his job, his kids, his interests, and his plans for the future are fair topics for conversation. What are the things you should not ask him about during your first chat?

- **His parents' occupations.** It may well come up on its own, but your asking could be seen as offensive, especially if your families come from different financial backgrounds.
- **His divorce.** While you are certainly entitled to know if he's been married before, you are not entitled to every detail of the breakup. Don't ask. You will know, eventually.
- **Exactly how much he earns.** It's enough to know that he is gainfully employed and/or extremely ambitious.
- **His debt.** Asking him about his FICO score and/or inquiring about the balances on his major credit cards

is out of line. Remember: There's a significant difference between being a mother and being a future mother-in-law. This kind of nosiness at this point in your relationship could keep this guy from ever warming up to you.

And then there are topics that may be very important to you but are generally divisive if you don't happen to hold the same beliefs. Don't broach the subject of politics or religion in your first meeting if you can help it. Give yourself a chance to like him for who he is first. Chances are if you're a card-carrying member of the GOP and he answers your question about his personal politics with "I'm a Democrat, ma'am," it's going to take a while to get over it if you've only just met the man. Conversely, if you get to know him before he unveils the liberal side of himself, it will be easier for you because you know he's a good person, political differences aside.

Meeting His Family

The MOB has to be prepared to make friends with the groom's parents for many reasons. For one thing, you may all end up planning this wedding together. For another, you're going to be related by marriage soon, which means you'll be running into each other at the kids' home for years to come. Lastly, engaged couples want to live their lives in a perfect world—which is difficult to do if they're worried about how their parents will interact.

Neutral Ground

If you have never met his parents prior to the engagement, try to find a neutral place for all of you to meet. Don't invite other parties; simply invite parents and the engaged couple. A restaurant in your town or their town is the most appropriate venue. Having this first meeting at your house could be uncomfortable. Meeting in a restaurant is the perfect way to break the ice.

Let's Be Friends

While some parents can come together and take an automatic liking to one another, it's not always that easy, especially when parents are from very different financial, religious, or social situations. It can be very hard to find a common ground on which to form a friendship.

 Essential

The truth of the matter is that your daughter shouldn't have to worry about how all of the parents will get along. No matter what differences you have, you're all adults, capable of making pleasant conversation.

You can be helpful by initiating conversations where necessary. If, for example, you find yourself eating dinner with the groom's parents (during which you're supposed to be getting to know each other), don't steer all your conversation toward your daughter or your husband. You already know them. Branch out. Ask the groom's parents about their hobbies or their work or their other kids. People usually open up (even to strangers) when they're asked about themselves. You can also broach a bevy of neutral topics: current events, the weather, and even the upcoming wedding.

It may be difficult for you to play the role of moderator here, especially if you're on the shy side, but one of your responsibilities as the MOB is to help your daughter bring everyone together.

The Other Side

Occasionally, an MOB will find herself tethered to a set of groom's parents whom she just cannot tolerate. Before you launch into a litany of their faults, make sure you're being fair to them. Things you're right to be irritated by are as follows:

- Off-color comments or jokes
- Nasty comments about the kids' engagement
- Boasting (about income, homes, cars, etc.)

You'll notice that there are quite a few things that didn't make the list. Tattoos, bad grammar, and questionable fashion choices are not good reasons to write off the groom's family. So don't do it.

Now . . . what if you're the one being judged unfairly? Instead of returning the snub, kill the snubber(s) with kindness. Responding to rudeness with kindness makes you look good and leaves the door open for friendship at a later date. You may feel as though you appear anxious for approval, but this isn't necessarily the case. You're really doing your part to get along with your daughter's future in-laws, whom you won't be spending that much time with anyway. Think of this as a very good deed.

The Mother of the Groom

Now that you have met the parents, you need to get ready to have a rather close relationship with the mother of the groom. Remember, this is her baby getting married, too, and she probably has a few ideas of her own for his big day. Weddings are not just about the bride anymore (like they used to be).

What Makes the MOG Happy?

To make the planning process easier, find out early on what makes the mother of the groom happy. What does this mean? It means finding out which parts of the planning process she and her family might want to take on, or if there is a specific aspect of the wedding she wants to be in charge of. No matter how the two of you hit it off at the first meeting, this is a relationship that is (hopefully) permanent. The wedding planning process will set the tone for your relationship with the mother of the groom.

Communication with the MOG

Once your daughter has given you the ground rules, always follow her lead. Your daughter will inevitably know more about his mother than you do. The wedding planning process, the budget, and who is in charge of what are topics for you and the mother of the groom to discuss.

Just like your plan to communicate with your daughter for the duration of the engagement, you should have a plan to communicate with the groom's mother. Communication with the mother of the groom during the wedding planning process will foster a better relationship with both your child and her future spouse.

Enlist Her Help

No matter what kind of relationship your daughter or you have with the mother of the groom, there are certain areas where you really should enlist the mother of the groom's help, such as:

- **Planning the rehearsal dinner**—This is usually a given, but not always! So be sure to ask about it.
- **Groom's cake**—You will need to see if his family likes the tradition of the groom's cake. If they are interested in the idea, find out if they want to do the groom's cake at the rehearsal dinner or on the actual wedding day.
- **Video presentations**—If the couple wants to have a fun video montage of their life at the rehearsal or on the wedding day, the two of you definitely need to coordinate this.
- **Flowers**—Very traditional etiquette dictates that the groom (read: groom's parents) should cover the cost of the bridal bouquet; boutonnieres for the groomsmen, ushers, fathers, and grandfathers; as well as corsages for the mothers and grandmothers. Most likely the mother of the groom will be the person you will want to speak to about this. They, of course, will be the

ones to cover any costs associated with flowers for the rehearsal dinner as well.

- **Miscellaneous expenses**—Items such as the officiant, marriage license, groomsmen gifts, alcohol, transportation for the groom and groomsmen's, and music are expenses traditionally taken on by the groom's family. However, as with all financial decisions, discuss this with the couple as well, as there may be different ideas as to who will be paying for what. In many cases, the bride and the groom will take on some of these expenses themselves. It all depends on everyone's financial situation.

- **Ceremony**—Depending on how large each of your families are, the processional and seating at the ceremony can be a very interesting task to take on. Consult with the mother of the groom to see which of her family members need to be included in the processional and how many rows of seating need to be reserved for their family members. This is an item often overlooked until the rehearsal, but it's something that should be thought about before then.

- **Dancing**—As you start to plan the reception, you will get excited and nostalgic while planning the father/daughter dance, but don't forget the mother/son dance. Make sure you ask both the mother of the groom and the groom about this special dance.

- **Music**—You want to make sure *all* of your guests will want to be on the dance floor. Find out from his mom what she thinks about the type of music that should

42

be played. This becomes an incredibly important task when bringing two different cultures together.

- **Family traditions and customs**—The mother of the groom is going to be the best person to contact to determine what sorts of traditions and customs his side of the family will want to integrate into the wedding. This is particularly important when it comes to the ceremony, food, and dancing.
- **Photography**—Be sure to ask his mother for a list of "must-have" photos that need to be taken for his side of the family.
- **What to wear**—This is a great opportunity to gain some footing with the mother of the groom. Chatting about fashion and what the two of you will wear that day is a great way to break the ice. It is important to make sure that the two of you are setting the tone on the day of the wedding.

In the end, keeping the lines of communication between you and the mother of the groom open will bring nothing but good will for years to come!

Planning with His Family

There is no way to plan a wedding without consulting the parents of the groom at some point. Communication with the groom's parents about the budget, the rehearsal, and a whole slew of other topics is imperative.

Budget Concerns

Though the bride's family once headed up most of the wedding and covered the bulk of its expenses, the reality of today's ceremonies and receptions is that the groom's family often pitches in on the cost (which means they also get to have a say in the planning).

If you're prepared to pay for the entire wedding, you may want to shut them out of the planning process entirely—but it's not a wise move. Remember, their child is entering into this marriage as well. If the in-laws want to take over certain aspects of the wedding, it's best to let them to avoid wedding-related spats and long-term hard feelings.

 Alert

It may be difficult for you to compromise on your idea of the perfect wedding to accommodate the groom's family's ideas. Decide early on which issues are worth fighting over and which aren't. And, of course, keep in mind that in the end, what the bride and groom want should matter the most.

Now, this isn't to say that you should give them the go-ahead to book a bunch of clowns to entertain at the evening reception. What it means is that all of you (the bride and groom included) will need to sit down and discuss what type of wedding this is going to be: the size of the guest list, the menu, the entertainment . . . everything.

Guest Lists

If you are planning to send Save the Date cards and the mother of the groom plans to have a whole separate reception in her state, you two will have a lot to discuss. The best idea is to open the lines of communication between you and the mother of the groom. Guest lists will play a large role throughout the wedding planning process, and traditionally the mother of the groom will take care of planning the rehearsal dinner. From the Save the Date to the brunch the day after the wedding, you and the mother of the groom will need to know which members of both sides of the family need to be invited to all of the festivities. If the mother of the groom decides to have a separate reception, don't feel frustrated or upset. This may actually keep the cost of the wedding down if she plans to invite only family to the "real" wedding-day reception.

Rehearsal Dinner Etiquette

The rehearsal dinner is a relatively new tradition in the long history of weddings. This North American concept was invented to help the relatives from each side get to know one another. Typically the groom's parents will pay for this event. With the blending of families and differing financial backgrounds, there are always exceptions to the rules.

Types of Rehearsal Dinners

Rehearsal dinners can be very informal or superformal, depending on what the bride and the groom want.

The first choice should always be made available to the parents of the groom. If they are simply not in any position to host a dinner for fifty, the bride and groom might be able to help offset their costs. However, it is not uncommon for the parents of the bride to foot the bill for this event, depending on the logistics and family backgrounds.

Whom to Invite

The wedding party (including parents and grandparents) along with their significant others, the officiant, and his or her spouse are always invited to the rehearsal dinner. An invitation to the rehearsal dinner may also be given to extended families, out-of-town guests, and, if possible, the entire guest list.

Family Traditions

Almost every wedding has some sort of family tradition included in it. If you think your family does not have any traditions, you can rest assured that your daughter's fiancé's family probably has some to spare. Your two families are coming together, and you need to be amenable to mixing customs. Some might be based on culture or heritage, and the others could simply be traditions your grandmother started decades ago. Again, remember that a wedding is all about two families coming together. When that happens, it means blending two cultures (even if your daughter and fiancé were living on the same street growing up!). Every family is different. Family traditions can range from the simple to the elaborate, depending on culture, heritage, and social status.

Cultural Traditions

Your daughter could be marrying the next-door neighbor's son or someone from a far-off land. No matter whom she is marrying, be sure to embrace not only her fiancé but also his or her family's cultural traditions. If her fiancé's family is quiet and reserved and does not want to include your family's traditions, don't push the subject. However, if his or her family is excited about your traditions, be sure to put effort into learning more about their culture and wedding traditions as soon as possible. Depending on their background and your daughter's and your soon-to-be son- or daughter-in-law's choices, their culture could very well change the entire landscape of the wedding. Some couples prefer a blending of cultures, and some love to focus on just one. Be sure to accept and support their decision.

Popular Cultural Traditions in the United States

There are large segments of the U.S. population that have very distinctive cultural traditions. Here is a brief list of some of the most popular cultural traditions that reflect either cultural or religious backgrounds. As these are just basic descriptions, you and your daughter should research and reflect on these traditions if her fiancé plans to incorporate one of the following:

- **Jumping the broom**—Jumping the broom is a tradition that some African Americans choose to incorporate into their wedding ceremonies. At the end of the wedding ceremony, the married couple jumps over a broomstick and the guests cheer. It has deep cultural and spiritual meaning dating back to when African Americans were enslaved in the United States and forbidden to marry legally. Jumping the broom in front of witnesses signified that the couple was in a committed relationship. The tradition is also associated with some African countries and the United Kingdom in the eighteenth and nineteenth centuries.

- **Chuppah**—if you are Jewish, there is a good chance you already know about a chuppah. However, if you have never attended a Jewish wedding, you need to know what a chuppah is and what it represents. It is typically considered a basic component of a Jewish ceremony. It is a structure made with four poles and a cloth "roof," symbolizing the home that the couple will create. This tradition dates back to the Hebrew Bible. Many Jewish families use cloths that have been passed down from generation to generation for the top of the chuppah. Some families just want the structure and are not particular about what it is made of. Be sure to ask about the fiancé's family's preferences if both of your families come from Jewish heritage.

- **Mandap**—A mandap is a structure (very similar to a chuppah) that is used for most Southeast Asian or Indian weddings. A mandap typically has, but is not limited to, four poles. It is typically a covered structure that is ornately decorated with colorful fabrics and flowers to reflect the colors of the wedding. Every mandap is different, and the tradition of the mandap dates back to Sanskrit texts.

- **San-san-kudo ceremony**—Traditionally, the san-san-kudo is known as the sake-sharing part of a Japanese wedding ceremony. Typically, the couple is not married until they share sake together and share it with their parents as a symbol of the two families coming together. Each person takes three sips of sake from three different cups. There are different layers of meaning behind this, including three sets of couples; three human flaws (hatred, passion, and ignorance), along with deliverance from the three flaws; and the lucky number nine.

- **Nikah**—For Muslim weddings, the marriage contract is signed in a Nikah ceremony. The groom typically proposes to the bride in front of two witnesses. The Nikah is signed, and then the marriage is legal in religious Muslim law. Typically, the couple will share a date or some other type of sweet fruit to symbolize the sweetness of marriage.

- **Leis and garlands**—In Hawaiian tradition, a lei is used as a symbol of love, respect, and "aloha." Most people think of floral leis; however, in most traditional Hawaiian wedding ceremonies, the garlands are made of greenery and are exchanged by the bride and groom. Some couples choose to also have their hands tied together by the officiant with what is called a "maile lei." Some brides use orchid leis as floral head wreaths as well. Floral garlands are also used widely in Southeast Asian and Indian ceremonies for exchanging during the ceremony.

- **Confetti**—The very traditional Italian custom is to give your guests tiny little bags of Jordan almonds to represent the bittersweetness of marriage. The couple generally distributes the candy to each guest (as much as humanly possible depending on the guest count of your wedding and the amount of time you have at your reception).

- **Changing dresses**—While your daughter might only want one dress, her fiancé could be from China, Japan, Korea, or another culture that incorporates a different type of wedding wardrobe. For example, in China it is traditional for a bride to change her dress three times. The Chinese bride will wear an embroidered red dress (red is considered to be a very lucky color in Chinese culture) during the ceremony. The bride will then wear a white dress for the reception and finally a going-away dress. Japanese and Korean brides are known to change outfits after the ceremony as well. If your daughter is Indian or is marrying an Indian groom, she will probably want to wear a sari for the ceremony and then change into her Western wedding gown of choice for the reception. Many cultures have very ornate and beautiful wedding wardrobes. Your daughter might want to wear just one or three!

Other Traditions

There are all sorts of wedding traditions that are part of American culture or other cultures that your daughter might want to use. Some are more traditional than others. Some of the most typical wedding traditions in the United States are the following:

- "Something old, something new, something borrowed, something blue, and a sixpence in her shoe"—This is in reference to what the bride should be wearing on the day of the wedding. The sixpence comes from British tradition. If you can't find a sixpence, place a dime in her shoe or a special coin from your family's history. Some people are able to combine something old, blue, and borrowed by wearing their grandmother's sapphire ring or blue garter. Something new could be the wedding dress. The tradition is believed to bring good luck to a bride who has all five elements when she walks down the aisle.
- Bouquet and garter toss—Many couples choose to throw the bouquet at the end of the reception to all the single ladies who are present. The one who catches the bouquet is said to be the next one to get married. Then, the groom is supposed to take the garter of the bride to throw out to the single men who are present at the reception. The man who catches the garter is supposed to then place the garter on the woman who caught the bouquet. These two traditions are not as widely used as they once were.

- Cake toppers—There are all sorts of different things that you can put on top of the wedding cake. Many couples decide to reuse their parents' or grandparents' cake topper.

CHAPTER 3

Money Matters

*M*oney can be a difficult subject when planning a wedding. Specifically, *whose* money is supposed to pay for *what*? You may have already perused some bridal etiquette books, and you may have broken into a cold sweat when you read, "The bride who comes from a proper family will indeed expect her parents to pay for the entire ceremony and reception. And it will be grand!" Don't panic. There's a new reality out there for parents who can't fathom dropping their life savings on a wedding.

Bride's Family: Traditional Expenses

For those of you who cling to tradition, you'll want and need to know what it is you're hanging on to, at least as far as this wedding is concerned. Once your daughter comes home and announces her engagement, start considering wedding finances. The wedding spending starts now.

Toasting the Happy Couple

The bride's family traditionally hosts the first engagement party, but this is not an obligation. If you choose not to host this event, make it very clear to those who are inquiring about the party. The MOG might be interested in hosting this event.

What does the engagement party entail, financially? That depends on whether you're planning a formal or informal affair. An at-home party is obviously cheaper (the food, the entertainment, the free use of your own home), but formal gatherings are also popular, depending on the bride and groom's style.

 Essential

You do not need to send formal, professionally printed invitations for an engagement party unless it's a formal event. Save that money for another wedding-related expense (there will be many). Store-bought invites will suffice for this occasion.

The cost of this party will also depend on how many guests you're inviting, which is entirely up to you. You'll want to include members of the groom's family, of course, but beyond that, you can invite the entire town—or no one else. Everyone you invite to the engagement party, though, must also be invited to the wedding.

The MOB's Bill

Relatively speaking, the cost of the engagement party is nothing compared to the cost of the actual wedding. What else does the bride's family pay for, traditionally? The bride herself usually pays for wedding gifts for the groom and her attendants and for the groom's wedding ring. Her parents are traditionally responsible for:

- The bride's dress (and, of course, the MOB's dress)
- Most of the flowers
- Musicians for the church and the reception
- Fee for the church
- Transportation for the wedding party
- Photographer and videographer
- Invitations
- Reception venue
- Food
- Drinks

You may think this is some sort of joke, but it's not. The bride's family really does cover all of these expenses in a traditional arrangement.

The amount of money the bride's family ends up shelling out is dependent on several factors: the type of wedding (formal, semiformal, informal), the size of the guest list, and how creative the bride and her mom are when it comes to cutting costs. These factors will vary from wedding to wedding and might not end up being as daunting as you originally thought they would be.

The Groom's Family

There they are, counting their riches and snickering over their good fortune at being parents of the groom (at least at this particular wedding). But hang on—these people have a few financial obligations of their own. The groom himself is usually responsible for wedding gifts for the bride and the groomsmen, the bride's ring, gifts for the groomsmen, and the honeymoon. His parents should take care of the following expenses:

- Officiant's fee
- Flowers: bride's bouquet, mothers' and grandmothers' corsages, boutonnieres for groomsmen
- Rehearsal dinner

"That's it?" you ask. "Where's the rest?" Well, in a traditional setup, you've already paid for the rest. Is this fair? Perhaps in the days of dowries and arranged marriages it was a suitable system. However, in contemporary times, the imbalance of the bride's family paying for the bulk of the wedding seems outdated. Tradition is sometimes overrated, wouldn't you say?

Budget for Today's Weddings

If you come from a conservative and traditional background, etiquette will play a huge role in budgeting your daughter's wedding. However, in today's economy and culture, your two families need to be on the same page to figure out what sort of budget will work and who will pay for what, as there are no hard and fast rules anymore. The reality of who assumes what expenses in a typical wedding is not always bound by tradition.

Common Sense

Today, more couples are waiting until they're a bit older and established in their careers before they get married. Where a bride was once either fresh out of college (or even younger) when she took her wedding vows, it's more likely these days to see a bride who has been out in the real world, having started her career already. As a result, she can typically afford to contribute to her own wedding—or perhaps (along with her fiancé) even pay for the entire thing. Your parents may have scrimped and saved for your wedding, but that is not necessarily the case for today's brides.

Another bonus for a bride who has the money to spend on her own wedding is that she can either go all out and plan an extravagant affair or go to the other extreme and plan a very simple event. Whatever the case, if the couple is bound and determined to pay for most of this wedding by themselves, don't wallow in guilt. If you want to contribute, they may accept or refuse. Don't push the issue. You don't want to end up fighting over expenses.

Alert

You shouldn't feel guilty about your daughter paying for her own wedding. It's not a matter of what you're *not* doing for her—it's about what she is able to do for *herself*, which is exactly the way women of her generation have been raised to think. You will be able to help in other ways during the planning process.

One Big, Happy Planning Session

What about the bride and groom who are able to pay for part of the wedding but are also expecting some help from one or both sets of parents? How do you go about splitting the bill three ways? Does it have to be exactly even? Who takes the initiative on which parts? You need to know if the groom's parents are even interested in making a major contribution to the wedding. First and foremost, it is up to your daughter and her fiancé to take care of asking his parents whether or not they can contribute anything at all. You don't want to be caught in an embarrassing situation by calling them and asking yourself. Then, one of several situations will present itself:

- You and the groom's family can simply hand your wedding contributions to the bride and groom, and the kids can go ahead and plan their wedding. This route is highly recommended to make sure they have the wedding of their dreams.
- The groom's family might agree to pay for certain aspects of the wedding (for example, they might want

to pay for the bar bill and the limousine—or any other expense of their choice).

- You might go ahead and plan the entire wedding and then accept payment from the couple and/or her fiancé's family.

What happens in the end will be the result of who trusts whom and who feels comfortable doing what. In other words, if you and the fiancé's family barely know one another, don't expect them to hand you a check for several thousand dollars a whole year before the reception.

Did Someone Say *Happy*?

Alas, what happens when three different parties converge in an attempt to pull off the wedding of everyone's dreams? Sometimes, the end result is a fairy-tale wedding; other times, the planning process is so nightmarish that the couple wishes they had eloped. It is your role as MOB to help your daughter navigate this process. You're trying to help her pull off the wedding she wants. Their family, however, may not be on the same page. If her fiancé's family is paying for part of the wedding, they may feel as though they've been given the green light to do whatever they want. You might end up playing referee.

While it's very difficult to set ground rules for adults who are contributing their own money in an effort to assist in the planning and lessen the financial strain on your pocketbook, it is possible to be tactful about the whole situation.

 **Essential**

Try not to judge her fiancé's family—or their intentions—too harshly. Everyone has different tastes. As long as they mean well, find a way to work it out without establishing a lifetime of hard feelings between the two families.

The Rules of Planning

Your job is to stay out of the head planner's seat (even if you really are the one who is doing all the legwork) and to not make all the calls for your daughter. Your daughter and her fiancé are the ones who need to express their wants and needs to their parents. After all, the money her fiancé's parents are handing over is really a gift to the happy couple—it doesn't belong to you, per se, even if its real purpose is to alleviate your financial burden.

You really shouldn't get involved in this particular matter until the bride gives you the go-ahead. Hopefully, she will have made the first foray into the topic with her future in-laws already. Once the couple has some idea of where his family stands on the issue of money as it relates to this wedding, they will either give you the green light to contact the future in-laws or let you know that you're on your own.

Taking Care of Your Guests

After you have planned the entire budget and the basics of the wedding day, you need to check again to make sure your daughter and her fiancé have not forgotten to budget for the little things to take care of the guests. The small details can add up to large amounts of money if you don't plan well. Most of these items really do depend on the type of wedding that you are having.

- **Save the Dates**—While everyone knows you need to send invitations, Save the Dates are really all about showing courtesy to your guests ahead of time. This little card or e-mail helps your guests to plan their budget and time around your daughter's wedding. Of course, your daughter's wedding party is going to know the date long before, but many guests will be planning their vacations six months ahead of time. Maybe they'll want to make your daughter's wedding a part of their vacation to save money. Save the Dates will definitely need to be included in your budget if your daughter is planning a destination wedding.
- **Hospitality gifts**—These are really a very important element if you intend to have a lot of out-of-town guests. This is the first thing that your guests will see when they come to the hotel and sets the tone for the wedding. You can do something simple with directions and information about the wedding weekend with a bottle of water, or opt for a fancier option like a cute bag filled with all sorts of goodies and fun gifts.
- **Transportation for guests**—If you have a lot of guests coming in from out of town, many will not be able to rent cars and will just take cabs. However, if you can incorporate it into your budget, having transportation for your guests to and from the hotel (at least) is a huge

way to really take care of your guests while they attend your daughter's wedding weekend.

- **Favors**—While favors might not be a necessity, they are a very special way to say thank you to your guests before leaving for the night. Favors can range from a cookie made by your favorite local baker to a gorgeous, silver-plated tray to represent your Italian tradition!

Finding the Money

Where are you going to get the money to pay for your part of this wedding, anyway? Years ago, it was common to hear about families saving for their daughters' weddings. But nowadays, a wedding fund is more likely to be something a daughter only hopes exists. If you're short an entire fund for the wedding, but you're planning on writing at least a check or two to cover some of the costs, you might have some ideas swirling around in your mind. Are they feasible?

Keep the House

Refinancing is probably not the best idea, unless you were planning on doing so before your daughter's engagement. Here's why: when you refinance your home, you get a check (and a lower mortgage rate—at least temporarily), which is great if you have big bills to pay (bills related to a wedding, for example), but you're trading the equity you already have. In most cases, you're essentially starting from square one, as though you just bought the house. This is just fine if you're not planning on selling anytime soon (you can kiss your profit goodbye if you try to sell right away), and if you don't fall into the habit of cashing in on your home's value every time you spend a little too much money here or there.

Home Equity Loans

Home equity loans can be lifesavers . . . or they can come back to haunt you. In this transaction, homeowners can borrow a percentage of the value of their home to pay off higher-interest loans or large debts. The interest on the loan is usually tax-deductible. Again, this may be a good way to go if you're careful with your money to begin with, but it isn't recommended to borrow against your home to pay off your wedding debt.

 Fact

Folks who refinance to pay off bills trade their equity in their home for a quick payoff elsewhere, which can lead to spending trouble if you're quick to say, "Well, I'm out of debt. Guess I can afford to spend some more!"

The advantage is that you're paying less interest on your wedding debt right now. The downside is that you're paying off this loan for thirty years. Also, if the loan exceeds 100 percent of the value of your home, the interest is not tax-deductible, which means you've entered into a standard loan. If you fall behind on your payments for whatever reason, you might find yourself packing your bags.

Cash or Credit?

Is it advisable, then, to pay cash for a wedding? Believe it or not, it isn't—at least not literally. While it is smart to set a budget and a spending limit while simultaneously deciding which areas of the wedding are priority issues (does your daughter want stretch limos for the wedding party and the families, or would she rather spend that money on an open bar?), it's not wise to hand over cold, hard cash to pay the bills.

Whenever possible, try to pay deposits by credit card, but keep track of what you're spending. Once you give cash or a check to a vendor, your money is out of your hands, and if there's a problem in the future (say, the caterer decides he'd rather use your money to take a vacation instead of feeding your daughter's wedding guests), it's very possible that you'll never see a refund. Conversely, if you've used your plastic, your credit card company will help you fight any bogus charges. The chances of your being reunited with your dough are much better in this instance. And of course, always, always get a receipt and put it away somewhere safe.

 **Essential**

Using your credit card carefully could help you out if there's a dispute with a vendor. However, it's incredibly unwise to use credit to go on a wedding-spending bender by purchasing items you'd never buy otherwise (like a $15,000 designer original wedding dress). Set your budget early on and stick to it.

Sharing the Burden

If you take a look at your financial status and realize you just can't swing $30,000 within the next year (which is the average price tag of today's wedding), it is time to just have the conversation about who is going to pay for what. Maybe you can pay for half of the wedding or just a small amount. You have to be realistic. You did not get to this point in your life to burden yourself with debt just because your daughter wants to get married. Your daughter probably knows you best and will already have a pretty good idea as to what you can actually afford. So take the time to figure out the wedding budget and who will be paying for what after you have assessed how much you can contribute. This will undoubtedly be better than going into debt and selling off all of your valuables!

Destination Wedding Expenses

How do the costs for a destination wedding differ from the costs for a typical hometown event? In truth, you may get off a little easier if the bride and groom can cover the cost of this wedding themselves. In order to make your decision on whether you're going to throw your hat (or your banker's or planner's hat) into this ring, you'll want some specifics.

The Low-Down on Destinations

A destination wedding is a wedding that takes place in a far-off location, whether that is a resort that specializes in such occasions or an out-of-the-way vacation spot that holds a special meaning for the couple. Weddings of this nature are becoming more popular with the current generation of brides for several reasons:

- They're different from typical weddings back home.
- They're often held in locations known for their beauty.
- Couples can make this an intimate affair without offending the extended family.

If your daughter has dreams of getting married on the beach, in the Alps, or on a dude ranch, she might be cooking up something creative for her wedding day. Though many brides opt to head for resorts that routinely host destination weddings, other brides want their wedding day to be as different as possible from anything else anyone has ever seen.

 Fact

Traveling to far-flung places requires *a lot* of thought. Does the bride really want to spend an entire day in the air to reach the altar? Does her foreign location have a residency requirement for marriage? Encourage her to do some very thorough research on her destination of choice.

Until you hear the final word from the bride on this matter, all bets are off. At the same time, don't assume that because she's talking about a destination wedding it's going to be a huge expense—she might be talking about driving to a little inn two or three hours down the road.

Your Obligation

Wherever this wedding takes place, you already know that the bride's family typically covers the bulk of the wedding expenses. However, when a bride and groom choose a destination wedding, they're usually held responsible for the cost of their own wedding. Why? Because getting married on a beautiful beach or in a mountaintop lodge or on a ranch is their choice. And as a result of the research they did to find this dream location, they'll know whether they can afford this venture or not.

The planning for this event may be more difficult (if they're headed where no bride or groom has gone before), or it may be incredibly easy (some resorts offer wedding packages complete with planners to take care of every detail). Your daughter and her fiancé should know what they're getting into before booking reservations.

Guest Responsibilities

Since destination weddings are a newer trend, there is still some debate over who should ultimately pay which of the guests' bills. Generally, everyone should plan on paying for their own travel expenses. Other expense decisions (such as lodging and food) should be made on a case-by-case basis. If the bride and groom can afford to swing this tab, they should give some thought to doing so. On the other hand, many destination brides argue that their out-of-town guests would be paying for their own hotel rooms if they were traveling to a traditional wedding in the bride's hometown, so there's no reason not to expect this of them.

There's logic to both sides of the discussion. The important thing is that no matter what the bride and groom decide, their guests should know the situation well in advance of making their decision to attend the wedding.

You Can Join Us Now

If your daughter has chosen a destination wedding, you may find yourself fretting over the fact that your family and friends may not be able to make the trip. The perfect solution? A post-wedding reception! Hang on, Mom. It may not be as perfect as you're thinking.

If the bride and groom chose to take their vows in a remote location because they wanted their wedding to be as intimate as possible, what kind of message does that send to the guests you're inviting to the after-the-fact reception? If they weren't privileged enough to witness the vows, why should they come running now to celebrate the union?

On the other hand, if the bride and groom had an extensive guest list for their destination wedding and only a handful of guests were able to attend, a reception at home makes sense. Guests may have already sent gifts, or they might bring them to this party. (Or they might not. Remember, guests are never obligated to give presents.)

Post-Wedding Reception Invitations

If you're hosting a post-wedding reception, you can go as swanky or as down-home as you'd like, though most of these parties tend to be cocktails-and-cake events. For a formal reception, you should send out formal, printed invitations at least a month before the party. The wording on an invitation to this party reads:

Mr. and Mrs. Timothy Tuttle

request the pleasure of your company

at a reception

in honor of

Mr. and Mrs. Harold Hart

on Sunday, August eleventh

Two thousand and thirteen

at two o'clock in the afternoon

Sarasota Yacht Club

Sarasota, Florida

If the groom's family is pitching in for this event, add their names below yours:

Mr. and Mrs. Timothy Tuttle

and

Mr. and Mrs. Mitchell Murray . . .

Post-Wedding Expenses

Keep in mind that when the wedding is over with, you will typically have additional expenses to address. Depending on who is writing the check, make sure you have gathered the funds from the appropriate family members and handled the disbursements to any vendors so the bride does not have to whip out a checkbook in her wedding gown or have to call from the airport with her credit card on the way to her honeymoon.

Wedding Vendor Expenses

In some cases, you will have some additional expenses at the wedding that you did not plan on. For example, you'll have to pay for the extra hour you felt you needed since the dance floor was still so full ten minutes to midnight. It's always good to ask what those expenses might be ahead of time.

 Fact

One very popular and typically unplanned post-wedding expense is your wedding album. You can always ask to prepay for an album for you as a parent and possibly spring for one for the groom's parents.

Another issue that may pop up in metropolitan areas is parking and valet expenses for your vendors. Be sure to keep this in mind and have a few extra dollars on hand to take care of these expenses as well.

Clothing

After the wedding, the bride may want to dry-clean her dress and stow it away for her daughter or sell it online or at a local consignment shop. Don't fool yourself for a minute thinking that cleaning your daughter's wedding dress will cost the same as cleaning your other dresses. Wedding gowns typically have so much detail or expensive fabric that dry cleaners have to handle the dress with extreme care, which comes at a higher price. If she wants it preserved, there may also be sewing involved, along with acid-free paper and a large storage box to pay for.

If the groom forgets to get his tux rental back in time, they will charge late fees. Try to avoid these unnecessary costs with proper planning.

Other Wedding Expenses

Always make sure you have an extra cushion of cash and your checkbook handy the day of the wedding. Emergencies can always pop up, and it's better to be prepared with extra cash in case something happens. You may want to invest in a wedding-day emergency kit, which includes sewing basics, common ailment medications (like sinus medication, ibuprofen, and antibiotic ointment), candy and energy bars, and anything else that you feel will help you and others feel more comfortable and prepared the day of the wedding.

Gratuity Basics

Make sure you properly thank the wedding professionals who helped to make your daughter's wedding day fantastic. Some professionals will already add a gratuity to their contracts, while others will leave it up to you. Be prepared and have checks written or cash ready in envelopes for all of these professionals on the day of the wedding.

Caterers, Facility, and Wait Staff

If your contract does not have a gratuity included, depending on the service they give, 10–20 percent of *food and beverage only* before taxes is traditional (no need to have a gratuity added for the rentals they provide for you). Remember, your catering services are normally 50–60 percent of your entire budget, and the caterers handle virtually all of the setup of your event (tables, chairs, linens, glassware, etc.), breakdown, and cleanup. If you feel your catering manager did a particularly great job with customer service, an additional gratuity of your choice is always fitting. Bartenders normally work the hardest the first two hours of the reception, and your bartenders will be the first people to take care of guests once they arrive at the reception site. Take note and consider an additional tip for them.

Depending on where the wedding takes place, the contact person for the facility typically ends up doing a lot of legwork for you (including recommendations and coordination of vendors that work at their facility). Their gratuity should be either in the reception facility contract or in the catering services contract. If not, a 5–15 percent gratuity should be sufficient. Some facilities do not allow a gratuity for the host/hostess; in this case, a thoughtful gift is appropriate.

Florist, Lighting Companies, and Decorators

A gratuity (not delivery charge) might be included in the contract for these vendors. If there is no gratuity specified, a 5–10 percent tip is standard (before taxes). Some florists will bring extra flowers to decorate in addition to what is in your contract; take note and tip accordingly. Depending on the size of your wedding, most florists will bring additional staff to help create your floral designs in a timely matter; this should be taken into consideration as well. Lighting companies and some décor rental companies will sometimes leave staff on site to be sure your event is trouble-free. A reasonable gratuity for their extra effort is always appreciated.

Religious and Civil Officiants

Religious and civil officiants are normally not tipped. If you have a personal relationship with the officiant or the church/temple where your ceremony is being held, consider a monetary charitable gift of their choice. Some officiants have a standard rate for services. If your officiant does not have a standard rate, consider an "honorarium," depending on your budget or affinity.

Civil officiants are hardly ever tipped, as most civil government personnel are not allowed to receive tips due to local law. Consider giving a small gift for the occasion (e.g., a gift certificate or book).

Musicians and DJs

Musicians (for both ceremony and reception), whether a band or disc jockey, might include a gratuity in their contracts. If not, consider a $50–$200 tip per musician and a 5–15 percent tip per DJ, depending on their involvement and overall contract price.

Beauty and Spa Professionals

If you go to a salon or spa, tip as you normally would (around 10–15 percent). If you have a contracted individual who comes to your home or hotel where everyone is getting ready (and a gratuity is not already included in the price of her services), the gratuity should be 10–15 percent of her contract price, as well as any parking expenses that she may incur.

Photographers and Videographers

A 10–15 percent gratuity is sufficient depending on their extra effort. A photographer's or videographer's assistant should be tipped appropriately as well. Some clients like to wait to tip these two vendors until they receive their proofs and/or videos. Keep in mind if you tip the day of the event, they will be more likely to pay special attention to the processing and to deliver the proofs and videos quickly.

CHAPTER 4

Your Responsibilities

*O*nce you start referring to yourself as the mother of the bride, you may want to be aware of your official (and unofficial) duties, of which there are many. As hard as planning a wedding can be, just remember it leads up to one big day . . . and then it's over. Don't lose sight of the other important things in your life while your head is somewhere in the wedding clouds, but try to enjoy this fleeting time while you can.

Traditional MOB Responsibilities

You're one woman who will wear many hats throughout the wedding planning process. Your real duty, regardless of the etiquette surrounding the issue, is to get involved as much as the bride wants or needs you to be. Along the same lines, if she doesn't want you involved in a certain area of the planning, your duty is to back off.

Typical Official Duties

If the bride and her mom work well together and the bride is looking for some assistance, the MOB usually:

- Establishes a budget for the wedding and the reception if she is making a large contribution toward the final cost
- Helps the engaged couple check out various reception sites and vendors
- Hits the bridal shops with the bride
- Assists in putting the guest list together and works with the groom and/or his family in this regard
- Helps the bridesmaids plan a shower (ideally, by providing a guest list and perhaps a little financial assistance—the girls should do everything else)
- Chooses a stunning dress, and lets the groom's mom know all about it so that she won't clash
- Attends parties given in her daughter's honor
- Lends a hand addressing and mailing invitations

- Shuffles guests' names around in an attempt to work out a seating plan for the reception (and then helps fill out the seating cards)
- Helps the bride get dressed for the ceremony
- Participates in the receiving line after the ceremony
- Helps make sure the reception runs smoothly

Many MOBs feel as though they were born to play this take-charge role; others take one look at the workload and hesitate to get involved. If you fall into the latter category, keep in mind that, ideally, you'll only have the chance to get involved in your daughter's wedding once, and you may regret passing on some of these opportunities after the vows are said and the rings have been exchanged. This is a once-in-a-lifetime chance to share this incredibly special time with your daughter.

 Essential

A wedding, of course, is meant to bring people together. If you and your daughter have been leading close but separate adult lives for several years, this is a great opportunity to reconnect with each other.

Unofficial Duties

Your unofficial duties mainly involve the things you do all the time, regardless of who is engaged and who isn't. A wedding tends to take over the lives of anyone who is involved in its planning, and with so much talk about dresses and menus, it's easy to let nonbridal and nonwedding events slip through the cracks.

Your other responsibilities, then, are to touch base with your engaged daughter every now and then and ask how she's feeling about her impending life change. Let her cry when she gets frustrated, and take time to talk about other important issues (such as how she plans on balancing her relationship with a busy career). Also, try to balance your relationships with other people with the wedding. These are not necessarily easy tasks to accomplish, but they are as important as any of your official duties.

What's Expected of You and When

Now that you know what your official duties are, take those duties and carry them into situations. Your time to shine as MOB is quickly approaching, but this is not a role you can simply jump into on the day of the wedding. Now is the time to prepare yourself for what lies ahead: the shopping, the guest list, the parties, the wedding, and the reception.

Wedding Preparations

If you're getting involved in the planning, you'll be a valuable asset to the bride and groom, evaluating reception halls, interviewing vendors, and keeping in contact with various wedding businesses. You may be called upon to work out details and sign contracts. Your best bet here is to educate yourself so that you can be an informed consumer; your next-best bet is to only work with vendors who are willing to meet your needs. Settling for a banquet hall that doesn't offer the services you're looking for just because you and the bride love its entryway is going to set you off sooner or later.

 Fact

> The bride may ask you to help out with shopping trips—including her registry. If she's never lived on her own, she may have no idea what she needs (the stainless steel set of pots and pans) and what she *doesn't* need (the silver candelabra).

In addition, you'll need to put a guest list together for your side of the family and be in contact with the groom's family regarding their guest list. You'll give them a number to work with, and tell them when you'll need the names. Make sure you have the correct number to avoid any potentially sticky spots. For example, if the groom's mother submits her list to you (and it's within her limit), you shouldn't call her and ask her to eliminate some of the guests because your math was off. It could well be that she's already told these people that they are invited.

Wedding Eve

Often, the wedding rehearsal is held the night before the wedding (otherwise, it's held several nights prior to the big event). Every member of the wedding party (this includes you) should be there, because this is akin to a dress rehearsal—no one wants to see bridesmaids wandering around during the ceremony because they have no idea where they should be standing or what they should be doing. Ditto for the parents of the bride and groom. Sure, you know how to walk down an aisle, but do you know what you're supposed to do once the ceremony begins? (No, you're not supposed to straighten her veil and poof her train—unless you're doubling as the maid or matron of honor.)

The rehearsal dinner follows the run-through of the ceremony. The groom's family normally takes care of the details surrounding this event, so all you have to do is show up and be charming.

Wedding Day

When the big day finally arrives, you'll be the bride's right-hand woman. She'll need you to help her prepare herself for the ceremony, which may include driving her to the hairdresser's, helping her with her makeup, and assisting her with the big dress. You'll also deal with various hired help and the bridesmaids, too.

Alert

This can be a very stressful time for MOBs. Don't take it out on the bride. She's stressed, too, and getting on her case is only going to cause major friction between the two of you. Try not to be too controlling here. Try to work at *her* pace.

At the ceremony, you will most likely be seated in the first row before the bride enters the building. After you are seated, take the time to look around at the results of all your planning and then sit back and enjoy the ceremony. When the ceremony ends, you'll exit directly behind the wedding party. At the reception, your job is to be a welcoming hostess and make sure that everything goes according to plan—or, if something's amiss, to take it up with the banquet manager.

How to Avoid the *Pushy MOB* Label

Despite your best intentions, you may hear your daughter complaining about how bossy you've become since her engagement. Your first reaction may be to chalk it up to the bridal stress that sometimes strikes young women on their way to the altar. While this explanation may account for part of the problem, be sure to take a good, honest look at your own behavior. There's a chance—and it's just a chance, mind you—that you're veering into controlling-MOB territory. Some moms really do end up carrying the entire burden of the planning all by themselves, and do a great job of it, but some moms make things extraordinarily difficult for everyone around them, including the bride. To find out if this is you, answer the following questions:

- Have you been picking out reception halls, planning menus, and choosing dresses without even consulting the bride on her preferences?
- Is the groom completely in the dark about his own wedding, even though he keeps asking questions and continuously offers his help?
- Have you seen your husband lately, or is he avoiding you until after the wedding?

- Do you feel like you're the only person who seems to be losing sleep, wondering if this wedding will turn out perfectly?

How can you avoid this syndrome? From the get-go, you need to decide how much of the planning you're going to take on and which duties the bride and groom will handle. Make a schedule for yourself so that you aren't trying to book twelve vendors in one week, and take a break from planning when it gets to be too much. If you start early enough, you'll be able to pace your planning so that it doesn't all pile up on you three months prior to the wedding date—when finding vendors with open dates will be difficult and trying to plan pre-wedding parties and a wedding simultaneously will be incredibly stressful.

Keeping Dad in the Loop

Keeping the family connected while you're busy planning a wedding can be a tough task, especially if you happen to be married to a man who'd rather hide in his den than discuss wedding details. But remember, he might have some ideas of his own to contribute, and since he's most likely going to play a big part in constructing the budget, it's best to make sure you two are on the same page.

The Budget

If you and your husband are paying for most of this wedding, you need to sit down and discuss how much you're going to end up paying. It's important to be in agreement about how much you will be spending on this event. If one of you is normally a big spender, you need to realize that you'll probably have to cut back on the shopping—at least for now. Otherwise, you could find yourself broke after paying for those purchases and your daughter's wedding.

Does He *Want* In?

If you're sitting at the dinner table and your husband is full of ideas for this wedding, let him join the planning. Even if some of his ideas are notoriously suspect (for example, if his last suggestion for a night out included taking a mime class), give him a chance to wow you with his brilliance. While many dads choose to leave all of the planning to the bride's mom, some men really do want to help out. Don't deny him the chance.

Including Your Ex

Maybe you and your former husband are best friends and you can't foresee a single problem with the two of you contributing your time and money to this wedding. Or maybe you can't stand the mention of his name, and as far as you're concerned, there's no reason to include him in the planning because it would be detrimental to everyone to have the two of you working together on this.

Since MOBs usually take the reins of planning the wedding, you certainly are not obligated to put yourself in a position that's only going to make your job harder. However, you are going to have to find a way to communicate with him on certain issues, such as his side of the guest list, and whether he's contributing to this wedding. He should also be filled in on the dates and times of the rehearsal and the wedding as soon as possible.

 Alert

> If you really, truly feel it's in everyone's best interest to have someone act as liaison between you and your ex, do it. It would be far worse for the two of you to revisit old arguments and force the bride to deal with *that* during her engagement.

If your divorce was really bad, you may feel as though even speaking to this man on the phone is impossible for you to do without developing a weeklong migraine. It's all right to ask your daughter to intervene, but be aware that she may accuse you of being juvenile. Ignore her accusation and hand over the task of communications with her dad to her.

Above and Beyond

While there are quite a few tasks that are traditionally expected of the mother of the bride, there are plenty of chores that you won't find listed in any etiquette book. As the wedding approaches, you'll have your hands full dealing with situations that are common to every MOB. Handle these situations with uncommon courage and you will earn the title of MOB Extraordinaire!

Oh, Those Bridesmaids!

Unfortunately, some brides find that their bridesmaids cause them so much trouble and heartache that eloping starts sounding like a good option. Whether your daughter has chosen family or friends to fill the chiffon dresses, there always seems to be at least one who chooses to be disagreeable about everything—the dress, the bridal shower, or even the date and time of the wedding.

 Essential

Be extra careful when dealing with a bridesmaid who is a member of the groom's family. If the bride can't appeal to her reasonable side, perhaps her own mother can. If that fails, you're free to approach her, but remember, your daughter has to deal with her for the rest of her life.

What can the MOB do to help in this situation? First, you need to let your daughter try to handle it herself. It's really best if she can appeal to this unreasonable maid woman-to-woman and settle things that way. If the attendant in question is persistent in her quest to drive the bride insane, go ahead and step in—as long as the offenses are serious enough.

There are few people in this world more intimidating than an MOB who's had it. It's an honor for a woman to be included in a wedding party. Reminding the offender of this fact, and of the fact that it's not her right to be included (which implies that she can easily be excluded), may be enough to stop her behavior.

Oh, Those In-Laws!

Another bunch who may vex your daughter before the wedding are the in-laws. While it's understandable that tensions are high before the wedding (and to be fair, you have to acknowledge that whether these people are truly involved in the planning or not, their child is getting married, too), sometimes the in-laws' behavior goes beyond the realm of what reasonable brides can tolerate.

A groom's mother, for example, may bitterly contest everything about the wedding. An MOG who isn't paying a dime for the event is much easier to deal with than one who is paying half the expenses. She may be irritating, but since you and the bride don't have to work out any details with her (other than the guest list), your exposure to her will be minimal. Let her go her own way, and you and your daughter can go yours.

Alert

If wedding-related financial issues between the bride's and the groom's parents can't be resolved, the bride may have to think about returning any money they've contributed and planning a smaller wedding. Assure her this *will* be worth it in the long run.

If your daughter finds herself dealing with in-laws who are paying for at least part of the wedding and they simply disregard all of the bride's wishes, is it right for you to step in? It depends on how bold you're feeling, and it depends on the groom's parents, too. If you suspect that there's no malicious intent on their part and that your daughter could very easily straighten things out by speaking to them, then stay back. On the other hand, if you know your daughter has already had arguments with her future mother-in-law, sometimes a "meeting of the moms" is in order. The groom's mother may be able to intimidate a young bride, but she doesn't scare you. Lay it on the line with this woman: This wedding is neither yours nor the MOG's, and the bride's wishes should be respected.

Oh, That Bride!

While this is supposed to be a wonderful time in your daughter's life, some MOBs notice a slight personality change. Or, truth be told, the personality change is huge—and it's horrific. Out-of-control brides wreak havoc on everyone in sight—their attendants, their siblings, their coworkers, their grooms, and even their mothers. Are you supposed to ignore this?

You're a mom. You've been looking out for your girl from day one. So what should you do? She's an adult and you can't exactly ground her from her wedding, but you can tell her that an engagement ring does not confer upon her the right to treat others with disrespect. You can tell her that her lousy treatment of you is unacceptable. She may accuse you of being mean. Calmly explain to her that you're being honest. She won't thank you for this advice (not until she has to deal with a bratty bride herself), but everyone else in her life will admire how levelheaded and rational you are—and they'll also applaud your fearlessness at confronting the abysmal bride.

Wedding Planners and Family Help

One of the best tricks in the MOB's bag is assistance. Even the best and most enthusiastic wedding planners rely on help (which is why they're the best and most enthusiastic), because one woman simply cannot do everything. You may find that your out-of-town daughter drops this wedding in your lap with one instruction: "Plan it." Or your daughter may not have any interest whatsoever in planning her wedding, but she knows that if you take care of the details, it will be beautiful. Either way, if this wedding has ended up on your to-do list, you'll need all the help you can get—with a few caveats, of course.

Recruiting Helpers

If you have a sister or a good friend who might be willing to help out, ask her. Planning a wedding is something that people generally get excited over, and most will be flattered that you would trust them to be of assistance. Give your helper the numbers of some vendors and ask if she can set up appointments; bring her along to check out the various sites and wedding professionals. You'll be bombarded with wedding information, and having someone to assist you can be helpful for a few reasons:

- She may ask questions you hadn't thought of.
- She may see something you missed (like water damage or a filthy kitchen).
- She may present a point of view you hadn't considered (for example, she may be vegetarian and find herself

looking at a menu without a single vegetarian or vegan option).

- She can help remind you of situations that may occur with your family that you are forgetting (like your cousins who will need a babysitter or a family member who might need assistance going up and down steps).

Her thoughts and opinions might well save you from making some big errors.

Professional Help

Can't find anyone who can help you? Your sister is 300 miles away and your friends are too busy. You asked your husband and he just laughed. Are you doomed to an existence of solitary taste tests, wandering from caterer to caterer? Then you need help, and wedding planners are your best bet!

Give some thought to hiring a wedding planner. These professionals know the territory and can usually lead you in the right direction. With your budget and style in mind, they'll find the wedding professionals to help create the wedding your daughter wants. Any planner who's been in the business for a while knows the local vendors and can advise you as to which ones are reputable and well worth your money. Your planner might even have a good enough relationship with some of them that he can cut you a deal for some services. Remember, brides are typically not repeat clients for wedding professionals, but wedding planners are (on behalf of their clients). Wedding planners are constantly sending business to the same vendors, as they know they will do a good job for their clients. If wedding professionals know you're coming with a wedding planner, they are going to want to do the best job to make sure they keep that wedding planner happy as well!

 **Question**

How can I find a good wedding planner?
If you have friends who have recently enlisted the help of a consultant, they can tell you about their experiences. Other places to look are websites where local brides recommend wedding planners, local wedding blogs, and the blogs of wedding planners (to see how creative they can be).

Once you have a planner in mind, schedule an initial interview to discuss your "dream plan" and your budget, and to get an idea of what the planner is like. Then decide whether you'd want to work with this person. Remember that wedding planners provide a whole range of services. You may be looking for someone to simply advise you in certain matters of etiquette, or you may be looking for someone to plan the entire event; you need to know if this particular planner offers the services you're after. Typically, most experienced wedding planners offer at least three different packages:

- **Full consulting**—This is when you need help with everything! Obviously a package like this is going to be the most expensive option. Full consulting will help you with everything from event concept to follow-up with vendors after the wedding is over. This will *typically* include finding out availability of venues and professionals, finding products and accessories needed for the wedding day, pricing, scheduling and attending meetings with you, etiquette advice, overall design concepts, negotiating contracts for you, as well as taking care of all of the logistics for the wedding.

- **Partial consulting**—Most planners will offer a midlevel package that will not provide the whole kit and caboodle like full consulting but will point you in the right direction during the planning process. Most partial planning packages will give you referrals to vendors and help with a few other items like etiquette or negotiating. Unfortunately, partial planning really varies from planner to planner, so be sure to find out the specifics from them.
- **Wedding coordination**—This is the most basic of packages. This will *typically* cover helping with a timeline and doing a walk-through of your venue(s) with your caterer to make sure everyone is on the same page. The wedding coordinator will be present for the rehearsal and will coordinate the day of the wedding.

This should go without saying, but every single package from a wedding planner should include helping with the rehearsal (if you end up having one) and coordinating the day of the wedding. If a professional you're considering doesn't include these two very basic items, you should continue looking! Keep in mind that every wedding planning firm is different—meaning they will have different packages available, different personalities, and different specialties. Be sure to read through their package offerings and their contracts carefully, and take a look at the websites and blogs to see if their style fits with what you and your daughter want and need.

When you set up your appointment with a wedding planner, you'll need to have an estimate of your total wedding budget and a list of questions, like the following, to get you started:

- How long have you been in business?
- How much (or how little) of the wedding will you plan?
- How many people do you have on staff?
- How many weddings do you plan per month? Per day?
- What's your fee? (Is it a flat fee or a percentage of the total cost of the wedding?)
- Do you have any references from recent clients?
- Will you have assistance on the day of the wedding?
- Have you worked at our venue before?

Don't be afraid to ask a lot of questions and get a conversation going with the planner. If you're hiring a wedding planner to put an entire wedding together, you need to know that the two of you can work well together and that you'll be able to communicate your ideas effectively. If you get the feeling that the two of you will be butting heads for the next several months (on your dime), walk away.

Nontraditional Wedding Basics

Today's modern bride is always looking to make her wedding different. Different does not necessarily mean offbeat; it just means she does not want her wedding to look like every other wedding that appears in magazines and online.

The Ceremony

More and more brides are traveling and getting to know (and falling in love with) people of different cultural backgrounds. Your daughter may not be marrying someone from another country, but she may have loved a ceremony tradition that she saw somewhere on her travels. Be open to incorporating these interesting traditions. Although no outside vendor may be needed for whatever the tradition may be, be sure to ask the bride about all of the elements that she wants to have and then discuss them with your officiant. Typically, most officiants are aware of many customs from other cultures and may be able to help you find other vendors to help incorporate these ideas. If not, wedding planners and the Internet are your best bets for help.

The Reception

There are so many options when it comes to nontraditional reception ideas. She may not want flowers as centerpieces, or maybe she wants a carnival theme (since that is where she met the love of her life). Whatever your daughter and her betrothed want, try your best to find the wedding professionals who can make it happen. Always ask your current local vendors for advice if you're running out of ideas. Interesting and different weddings are how wedding planners came about. If you get stumped, call a wedding planner for an hour-long consultation (if you cannot afford a planning package).

Ideas for Nontraditional Weddings

The best place to find ideas for nontraditional weddings is online. With the influx of so many wedding blogs and websites and Pinterest (*www.pinterest.com*) comes a never-ending amount of inspiration and ideas for your daughter's wedding. Be sure to ask your daughter what her style is and if there are any blogs that she is currently drooling over so you can be on the same page with her. Here are a few ideas to get your creative juices flowing:

- **Ceremony ideas**—Their wedding does not have to be in a place of worship or a garden. Many couples are opting for ceremonies with interesting backdrops that take place in the same venue as the reception to make things easier for guests. Think about a gorgeous set of stringed lights as a backdrop for the ceremony inside the barn where the reception will be. Another idea is to have the ceremony in another gallery if the reception is in a museum or art space. You can transform almost any space into a gorgeous ceremony setting that reflects the couple.
- **Wedding style**—Gone is the idea of brides only being able to wear long, white dresses with veils and trains. Many brides are opting for dresses with colored sashes or dresses that do not fall in the white-to-champagne

spectrum. More and more brides are choosing soft pinks, golds, and shades of blue for their dresses. Some brides are designing their own dresses or pant suits to reflect their personal style. Many grooms are also ditching tuxes for more comfortable suit and vest options.

- **Reception ideas**—While it would be nice for everyone to have a surf-and-turf dinner at the local country club, your daughter may be thinking something totally different. Budget might play a role, or it could just be your daughter's personality. Maybe she wants to get married at the summer lake house and have a simple backyard BBQ, complete with rods for guests to fish off the dock and a tub full of locally brewed beer. Cocktail receptions are also on the rise, with less formal food that is more than enough to fill the guests up. Think stations with local cheeses, pasta and salad stations, and mini cheeseburgers.
- **Dessert ideas**—Your daughter might be living a gluten-free life or simply just does not like cake. Instead of a wedding cake, she might want a fun dessert bar filled with everything from cupcakes and tarts to her favorite candy. Or she might be pie lover and want all of her aunts to bake their trademark pies for the guests to choose from. Don't limit your daughter to just a three-tiered wedding cake.

Every single aspect of the wedding can be different. The main idea of having a nontraditional wedding is to have an event that truly reflects your daughter and her fiancé!

CHAPTER 5

Wedding Planning 411

*I*t takes certain inquisitive skills to plan a wedding. There's good news and bad news here. The good news is that the wedding industry on the whole is huge, and you'll most likely be able to find just about every service you're looking for. The bad news is that it's going to take a lot of effort from whoever is in charge of planning. Get some rest, and then start pounding the pavement (or consider getting a wedding planner).

Your Timeline and Plan

You may feel as though you're going to get an education when you sit down to discuss the particulars of this wedding with certain vendors. That's not the case. You should go out of your way to educate yourself before you meet face-to-face with a banquet manager, baker, or florist. You don't want to be hit with sticker shock while you're interviewing a vendor, and you definitely don't want to end up paying too much for anything.

Pass It On!

One of the best ways to get a line on who's reputable, who isn't, and which vendors offer the best services is through word of mouth. You can start asking around as soon as your daughter has some idea of what type of wedding she's leaning toward. Don't worry if you don't have any close friends or family members who have recently gone through the wedding process. You can find plenty of advice online at some of the bigger and more local websites. Blogs and local magazine websites tend to have some of the best advice for those beginning their wedding planning process. Some of the bigger wedding planning websites will let local brides talk about their vendors after the wedding as well.

The Internet is especially helpful for finding the latest trends in weddings. For example, if your daughter just has to have exotic wildflowers at her reception, you can send an e-mail with photos from a particular website to the florist before you meet. This way you can see (ahead of time) whether or not she is capable of reproducing such glory. Remember to organize your information and to take a notebook (either paper or your laptop) along with you. You'll have a lot of information thrown at you. In order to make the best decision, you'll have to sort through prices and services at some point, which is going to be difficult to do if you haven't organized your information.

 Fact

You'll want to get a good idea of what things should cost before you start making appointments with various vendors. Start looking online in order to get a general idea of what vendors are charging before you meet with them. E-mail or call them about pricing before meeting with them as well.

Learn by Example

One last way to do your research is to start making the reception rounds. This will give you a good idea of how a reception venue really handles several hundred guests. Most banquet managers and other vendors will give you dates and times so that you can see their work in progress. Try not to infringe on other brides and grooms to satisfy your interest. Go to the reception site about thirty to forty-five minutes prior to the wedding or reception starting. This way you can see how things look in person but not interrupt or take away from someone else's perfect day.

What Are You Getting Yourself Into?

Once you've met with the vendors, you'll narrow down your choices, and at some point you'll want to negotiate with them. Be aware that you're really not in a position to negotiate, because most reputable vendors (especially in the busy wedding months, from April to October) have all the business they need. They don't need to give you a break, because there's usually someone else in line right behind you who's willing to pay full price.

 **Essential**

If you're planning an extraordinarily large wedding, you might be able to negotiate a lower price per head with a banquet hall or caterer due to the sheer volume of business you're offering.

The most popular wedding and reception sites are often booked solid a year to two years in advance, so you may feel as though you're under the gun even if you've got an early start in your planning. Don't let pressure blind you. Take a good look at what you're being offered by various vendors and what you're going to end up paying for. Don't sign a contract until you're completely comfortable with the terms of it.

Eco-Friendly Options

Being green is a growing trend in the wedding industry, but there are still several areas in the United States (and around the world) that are behind in green concepts and practices. Be proactive and try to look for ways to be eco-friendly. Who knows, you might actually help a vendor to start using green practices by simply asking about them!

Questions to Ask

There are a lot of questions that need to be asked of vendors to find out if they are truly eco-conscious. Here is a basic list of questions to keep in mind when meeting with vendors to determine how green they are:

- **Where are your supplies made and/or shipped from?** Because using local resources keeps carbon emissions down, green brides and MOBs know it can be extremely wasteful to bring in items from faraway places.
- **Do you belong to any green associations?** In most major metropolitan cities, there are associations and groups that help educate vendors and businesses on how to stay or become green. Many businesses can even become "certified green," a special status designated by different agencies. There are some associations that have green awards and some local newspapers and magazines that cite the best green businesses. Find out if your vendors have any green awards or articles written about their eco-friendliness.
- **Are you doing any community outreach or conservation efforts?** Being green is way more than just trying to conserve energy and protect the environment from

chemicals and waste. Having an eco-friendly company is also about community outreach and creating a greater good. For example, find out if your caterer donates time and energy (or money) toward local community groups. Keep in mind that some vendors don't have enough staff or time to actually be proactive and hands-on with community outreach, so if they are donating to great causes in your area, that's a wonderful start! Their "community" may reach far beyond the county lines. Maybe they are giving to a global fund for planting new trees or giving a portion of their proceeds to carbon offsetting. Find out what causes your vendors are involved with.

 Alert

Some companies are "greenwashing," meaning they say they are eco-friendly when they are not. Research online to find out which vendors are actually making a difference in the environmental area.

Easy Ways to Be Green

There are a number of simple and easy ways to make sure your daughter's day is greener. Here are a few examples:

- **Buy a used wedding gown.** This may sound daunting, but there are tons of places online to buy one-of-a-kind (and couture) wedding gowns at a fraction of their original price. Not only are you reusing a dress (that has only been worn once and is in perfect condition still), but you also get to save money at the same time.

- **Book a nonprofit venue.** There are tons of venues that are run by the government or nonprofit organizations that give back to the community. Places like nature sanctuaries, city gardens, and historical mansions help protect the environment, educate the community, and preserve and maintain buildings.

- **Rent shuttles for your guests.** If you have a large number of guests coming in from out of town, try to rent shuttles to and from hotels to help reduce the amount of carbon emissions for the wedding.

- **Keep it local.** Try not to invite too many out-of-town guests, and only hire vendors that are local. Also, ask your caterer to use local produce and meats to keep their carbon emissions down as well.

- **Nix packaged favors.** Keep favors simple. Try not to order favors online; instead, use a local provider of interesting favors. Examples include fruit and honey from local farmers or something interesting from a local artisan. (Another option is to not do favors at all.)

Ceremony and Reception Basics

Many brides still opt for a traditional religious wedding, while others look for a nonreligious site. No matter what your daughter's choice, you will have a wider range of possibilities for the reception. Ask her questions about the type of wedding she wants before you embark on finding these two distinct venues, as they will shape the rest of the wedding details and decisions.

Religious Versus Civil Ceremonies

Depending on whether your daughter wants to get married in a church, temple, garden, ballroom, or the courthouse, you will have numerous options to choose from—or only one! If she wants to get married in the church she grew up going to or in the temple where he worshipped, then you have your answer. However, many couples opt for a civil ceremony in a simple garden setting or in the hotel or mansion where the reception will be.

 Essential

If your daughter and her fiancé decide to have an Indian/Hindu ceremony, it is important to find out from the ceremony location if they will allow open flames. Indian ceremonies almost always require the element of fire.

No matter where they decide to get married, you will need to find out the limitations and what will be provided by the venue. If it is not in a place of worship, you will have to think about chairs, any small tables you might need, and audio equipment. The upside to having a wedding at a civil spot is that the reception can be held there. Having the ceremony and reception in one location will reduce the need for shuttle buses, and there will be no delay between the ceremony and the reception.

Onsite Catering

If the reception is scheduled to take place at a reception facility (hotel, club, or restaurant), you will be working with their onsite staff. Some of these places will let you bring in your own caterer, but many won't. Meeting with an onsite catering manager should be a fairly pleasant experience. It's this person's job to inform you about the site and the services offered there. Most places have a wide variety of packages, ranging from cocktail receptions to seven-course dinners and beyond, so you should be able to find what you're looking for.

 Essential

Be sure to request a tasting. You're going to be shelling out quite a bit for some good eats; you shouldn't be expected to choose the menu without knowing what's to your liking and what isn't.

The manager will give you a tour of the facility, making sure to highlight certain areas (the terrace, which is perfect for pictures, or the lush and private bride's room) and hoping to grab your attention (and your business). What will probably be most important to you and the bride is whether a certain site can meet your needs, whether they can come close to your price, and, simply, whether you like the facility or not.

Some things to ask about the location:

- How many guests can they handle comfortably?
- Is the dinner a sit-down affair? Do they offer a buffet option?
- Where will the band or DJ set up? Where is the dance floor?
- How will the staff dress? How many servers will there be?
- Will your head count have to include vendors? If not, what is the price for vendor meals? What will they serve?
- Can the site provide a cake, or will you have to find a baker? Is there a cake-cutting fee for outside bakers?
- Is there an extra fee for a champagne toast?
- What is the cost of an open bar? How many hours does the price include?
- Is there an extra charge for valet parking or a coat-room attendant?
- How much of a deposit is required? When is the full balance due?
- Are there any other fees?
- Do they provide diabetic, vegetarian/vegan, and gluten-free meals?

If you don't like what you're hearing, but you love the actual surroundings, close your eyes and think. It's not worth the money you'll spend if the place is short-staffed, if your guests will be squeezed into their seats, and if it costs extra for nice table linens. The reception is usually the most expensive part of a wedding; make sure you're getting what you want from the deal.

Offsite Caterers

If the bride and groom decide to take their wedding on the road, you'll have to find someone to follow—with chafing dishes and food. Most metropolitan areas have caterers just for this reason, and if you find that there is not a caterer in sight, ask around and find the best restaurant to cater it for you.

When you've found someone who specializes in the type of event you're planning (be it formal, semiformal, or informal), you'll have to make a few inquiries. You'll want to know how long they've been in business, what size events they normally handle, and whether they can provide you with references from other weddings they've done. You'll want to make sure they have any permits that are required by law and ask if they're insured. Ask about deposits and final payments, as well as the cost of the bar and when the final head count is due. Be sure to inquire about any additional time they might need for setup and breakdown at the facility and the cost of any additional rental equipment.

Keep in mind that if you're hiring a caterer for an outdoor affair, you may also need a tent, which is an added cost (and most likely will necessitate your dealing specifically with a tent company).

The Cake

Looking for the perfect wedding cake hardly seems like a chore—they can be elegant, whimsical, and most important, they're delicious. The bride, however, will have very specific ideas about what she will and won't accept, which makes this transaction almost as labor-intensive as finding the right place for the reception.

 Alert

Take climate into consideration when ordering a cake! No one wants to eat a runny cheesecake or a droopy fruit-filled confection at a patio reception on a hot August day. The cake will look and taste horrible if it melts.

First of all, you'll need to find someone who specializes in wedding cakes. This is one confection you don't want to leave to chance. If you don't know of a wedding-cake business in the area, ask around and search online. Most cakes are not only the dessert for the reception but also part of the décor!

When you go for a cake tasting, talk about price before you get into discussing the most elegant cake the baker can create for you. A wedding cake is typically priced by the slice, and the price of the slice is based on what it contains. A base price is usually for plain cake with buttercream frosting. As you add to that slice (fillings, upgraded frosting choices, unusual design work), the price rises accordingly. For example, if a plain cake costs $4.50/slice, but your daughter wants a fruit filling and fondant frosting, you'll probably pay several dollars per slice above the base price. If you have no idea how much cake you'll need, ask the baker. Most will advise serving 3- or 4-inch slices. If in doubt, err on the side of caution—you don't want to run short on cake!

Other matters to discuss when interviewing the baker:

- Is delivery included in the price? What if the reception is outside of the delivery area?
- Can fresh or silk flowers be added to the cake or placed in between the tiers? Do you provide flowers, or can the florist provide them to match the other décor?
- If the cake is destroyed before or during delivery, will another cake be available for the reception? Will there be a price adjustment if it's a less expensive substitution?
- What time will the cake be delivered to the reception site?

Some receptions include a pastry table (or an entire room filled with goodies) later in the evening. If you're planning on doing pastries in addition to the cake, consider having a smaller cake, as some of your guests will gravitate toward other sweets. If you don't want cake and prefer something fun and interesting, opt for a dessert or candy bar that will have various options with a variety of sweets ranging from cake and pastries to your favorite candies in jars. Caterers and planners will be your best bet in figuring out how to make a dessert or candy bar happen for you.

Photography and Videography

Pictures and videos are one area where brides and grooms are sometimes willing to contribute their own resources. After the wedding has come and gone, the images of the event will last a lifetime. Finding the right photographer and videographer sometimes takes a bit of effort. Ask around, and research online. If possible, try not to choose the least expensive vendor, because the discounted price may indicate a lack of experience. However, all professionals have to work their way up, so you may not need to find someone who has been in the business for thirty years.

Finding the Right Photographer

You'll have two choices when looking for a wedding photographer: working with an independent photographer or working with a studio. (There's actually a third, inadvisable choice, which is hiring a friend or family member to take photos. Unless this person is a professional photographer, don't do it. If the pictures turn out badly, you'll be forced into a confrontation that will never be resolved, because you and the bride will mourn the loss of those pictures forever.)

There are some differences between independent photographers and studios. The biggest difference is that an independent photographer will be the one to show up to take the wedding pictures. With a studio, you may not know who will be entrusted with the task. If you want to work with a particular studio because a friend has recommended the place to you, get the name of the photographer she dealt with. If the studio can't guarantee the same photographer, or even a specific photographer, think about taking your business elsewhere. You want to see this person's work, and you want to know that he or she has experience with weddings.

 **Essential**

Good photographers are in high demand. Start looking around as soon as you can, and if you just love someone's work, don't wait to book. His or her schedule will be filled before you know it.

What to Ask Your Photographer

After you've narrowed down your choices, you'll have to interview the photographers yourself. You'll want to know how long they've been in business and what their background or training is. You should ask if they specialize in weddings or whether they work in a studio. Be sure to carefully consider the organization of the photos that are in their sample books. Do they include a variety of people (the wedding party and most of the guests), backgrounds, and activities (posed and action shots, candid and group shots)? Are all of the important points of any wedding day (the exchange of vows, the kiss, the cake cutting, the toasts, the dancing) captured in the pictures before you?

Ask about their packages and albums and consider the types of albums they are offering. Are they creative? Modern brides want something different, and they want to make sure they can use the photos in different ways after the wedding. Most photographers are using digital photography and can offer a disk of the photos after the wedding. Some will post the photos online. Some will make brides pay for the digital negatives, so be sure to ask! If your daughter is not interested in an album but you are, make it known. Some photographers do not deal with albums, and you might be left to create an album on your own.

The Video

Videographers may be affiliated with photographers; or they may be independent contractors. You'll want to know how many weddings they've filmed, and you'll want to see some of their most recent work. Get some references and call them. Ask about the equipment (you should hear the terms *digital*, *HD*, and *DVD* being thrown into the conversation) and editing techniques: Do they include titles in the finished product? How about music or special effects? What does each package include? How many copies can you order and how much will each cost? How long will it take to receive the final, edited version? Will they give you all the unedited video as well? Do they provide a highlight film that tells the story of the day?

Videography is something that becomes more technologically advanced every day. When you think you only need photography, consider the fact that video will allow later generations to experience this amazing day and to hear their relatives' voices.

Entertainment

You'll need to entertain your guests before, during, and after the ceremony with music. You may hire separate musicians for the ceremony, the cocktail hour, and the reception, or you may call on the same group to do double (or triple) duty somewhere. You may want to also consider other forms of entertainment like dancers, cigar rollers, caricature artists, and beyond!

Music for the Ceremony

Are you looking for a soloist, an organist, a string quartet, or a guitarist? If you are having a religious wedding, check with your religious officiant first to make sure that the music your daughter wants is allowed. Some religions demand that the music during marriage ceremonies be religious; others allow secular music as long as it meets certain criteria.

Next, you'll need to track down the perfect performers. If your daughter loves organ music and your church already has an organist, your job is fairly easy. However, if she's looking for a topnotch soprano or a professional string quartet for the ceremony, try contacting a music talent agency that represents bands and musicians.

Reception Music

For most brides and grooms (and MOBs), the question of the reception music comes down to two choices: a band or a DJ. Some people find that they have a strong preference from the get-go and would never consider the alternative, while other folks really try to weigh the pros and cons of each.

Even if someone gives you the name of the best band or DJ in town, it's important for you to hear them before you sign a contract with them. Picture the guests who will be at your reception and ask yourself if they will enjoy the type of music you're listening to. How does the bandleader or DJ handle his emcee responsibilities? Is he dignified enough for your crowd of friends and relatives? What about his apparel (and that of the band)?

 Fact

Generally speaking, a live band is always going to be more expensive than a DJ. DJs are completely acceptable at a formal reception, and it is not unreasonable to ask that your DJ be appropriately dressed (and that it be put in writing).

If you like what you hear, but the playlist isn't quite perfect for your daughter's wedding, ask if the band or DJ has an entirely different set that is appropriate for other occasions.

If you're almost won over, take the time to schedule an interview and discuss other options. A good band (or DJ) is not always easy to find, and since the best guys are booked more than a year in advance, this is not a task you want to leave unfinished for too long.

Other Entertainment

Weddings are becoming more like major productions. A wedding is not the ceremony followed by food and cake anymore. Brides are opting for more pizzazz at their receptions and wanting more than just music to entertain. Other popular options include:

- Asking your photographer to set up a photo or video booth to salute the bride and the groom

- Asking your wedding planner or caterer to set up a candy bar
- Bringing in cultural dancers to represent your culture or his family's heritage
- Setting up a lounge area for guests to smoke cigars
- Creating a tea-tasting station that represents the teas of the world that the bride and groom love

The options are truly endless, as every couple is unique. Ask your daughter and her groom what their favorite hobbies are and try to incorporate them into the reception.

Flowers and Décor

Décor and flowers are really what personalize the ceremony and reception space. There is so much more to decorating a wedding reception than the centerpieces on the tables.

Floral Designs

When meeting with a florist, you may be in need of only a few key items that most brides need (like the bridal bouquet, altar arrangements, and centerpieces). However, if you are having a much more complicated event due to your culture and blending of two families, you will want to make sure the florist can meet your needs. If you want lighting, draping, garlands, lanterns, and the works, be sure to e-mail or call about these items before making an appointment. Your best route is to find a floral designer who has access to all of these items.

Some questions you should ask when meeting with a floral designer are:

- Are your flowers grown and purchased locally (essential for an eco-friendly wedding)?
- How much time do you need for setup?
- Do you set up and break down everything?
- What are your delivery fees?
- How many personnel will be on site for setup?
- When can we give you the final guest count for centerpiece purposes?
- Do you offer rental vases and props?

There are some basic bits of information your florist will need to know before your initial consultation. You will need to know the color scheme your daughter wants. This includes the color of her bridal gown and bridesmaid dresses, the types of suits and colors of ties (or ascots) for the groom and groomsmen, and the linen colors for the reception. In addition to knowing the colors for the day, you will need to have the venues booked and know the estimated number of guests you plan on having. Your florist will only be able to give you an accurate proposal and ideas for floral designs for your budgeting purposes if you have all of this information. Have a good idea of what you want to spend before you go to this meeting as well. You should expect to spend 7–10 percent (sometimes more if you are in a major metropolitan area) of your overall budget on flowers. Décor items like structures, lighting, and props will be additional expenses.

Other Décor Items

Some floral designers can provide only flowers, as they do not have the storage available for larger rental items. If you are having an Indian wedding, you might want a mandap, or if you are Jewish, you will want a chuppah. Not all florists can provide these items. Does it make sense to have two different florists provide different floral designs the day of your daughter's wedding? The answer to this is maybe, but it will make your planning efforts more difficult. If you need lighting, tenting, draping, and props in addition to flowers, and the florist is unable to provide these items, see if they can recommend a rental company that they like working with. It will not only make your job easier, but it will simplify their job as well.

Transportation

When all of the major vendors are in place, be sure you know how your daughter, as well as the entire wedding party, is going to get to the ceremony. You also need to ensure that the guests will arrive on time.

Wedding Party Transportation

If most of your wedding party is local, it is not out of the question to have them drive themselves to the ceremony and reception. Depending on how formal the wedding is and how close in proximity the reception is to the hotel where everyone is staying, you may be able to get away with providing special transportation just for the bride or driving her in your sister's Mercedes. However, if your daughter has more than three or four attendants on both sides of the aisle, you may find it easier to keep the wedding party on schedule by having one limo for the bride's side and one limo for her fiancé's side available. When it comes to you and the father of the bride, why not take a luxury car to the ceremony and to the reception? Her fiancé's parents will probably need transportation as well. Adding a couple of luxury sedans to a limo contract may only be a fraction of the cost of the limos and well worth the peace of mind!

Guest Transportation

It is not uncommon these days for the bride and groom to provide shuttle transportation for their guests if they have a large out-of-town contingency. However, if you are having your reception at a hotel, try to advise the guests to stay at that hotel or close by. A quick cab ride is not going to hurt a guest's feelings. You will find that if a guest is willing to attend your daughter's wedding, he or she is willing to find a way there. However, if you have a lot of guests coming from out of town, it is common courtesy to find some sort of transportation for them, especially if the hotels you have chosen are far from your ceremony and reception sites.

Accommodations

Whether you are having an out-of-town wedding or a wedding just across town, you may have to consider accommodations, not only for your guests, but also for your daughter and her bridesmaids on the day of the wedding.

If there are ten bridesmaids in the wedding party, will they all fit in your living room on the day of the wedding?

The Guests

Depending on where your daughter plans to have her wedding, you may have to consider booking a block of rooms for your out-of-town guests. Whether you are having 10 or 200 people coming from out of town, you will need to work with a hotel that is close to your reception spot.

Some hotels will require a deposit for blocking a large amount of rooms, and some will let you block rooms in payment plans. Be sure to ask questions about the hotel block contract you are signing. Some hotels may not be able to accommodate all of your guests, and some of your guests may not be able to afford the price of an expensive hotel. Make sure you have at least two hotel options for your guests, and be sure at least one is budget-friendly.

 Alert

While some hotels do offer a better rate for wedding blocks, don't assume that the rate you have negotiated for guests will be the cheapest. Some hotel rooms can be found cheaper online even up to a couple of weeks prior to the wedding.

Wedding Party Rooms

Your home may be like Grand Central Station for the wedding (phone-wise), but it does not have to be filled with people on the day of the wedding. If the thought of having all the bridesmaids getting ready at your home fills you with anxiety, you should consider reserving a large suite at the hotel you have booked (or one close by the ceremony and reception sites). You could also have an expert hair and makeup professional come to the hotel room to assist the bride and bridesmaids.

The groom and his groomsmen typically don't have to spend as much time getting ready as the bride and bridesmaids. They might stop by the groom's suite on their way to the ceremony site, but it is not necessary to get another large suite for the groom and his groomsmen.

Details

Other small details will come into play that you will have to remember for the wedding. Programs, menus, table numbers, escort cards, place cards, favors, accessories, the guest book, and any other personalized items like drink stirrers and cocktail napkins must be taken into consideration to add the final polished touch to your daughter's special day.

Stationery for the Ceremony and Reception

After the final menu has been confirmed and your daughter has had her final meeting with the officiant, prepare the printed items needed for the ceremony and reception. Try to get your menus and programs printed at least two weeks prior to the wedding to avoid paying a rush fee. Other paper items you must consider are escort and place cards, bar menus, table names and numbers, and any other signage your daughter may want to showcase at the wedding. Don't forget a guest book, which could be anything from a book to a photo of the couple in a matte frame to a Polaroid station. You may also want to consider paper cocktail napkins, especially if you don't want the venue logo on your napkins during the cocktail hour.

Nonpaper Essentials

Other important nonpaper essentials at most traditional weddings include cake knives, toasting glasses, unity candle sets, emergency and first-aid kits, and favors. If you are having a nontraditional or multicultural wedding, there is a long list of other items that you may need to get together. Some examples include:

- **Jewish wedding essentials**—Kiddush cup, tallis or tallit, wine, Ketubah with an easel, and a glass to break for the ceremony alone. If you end up having a Tisch before the chuppah ceremony, you will need a plate to break as well.
- **Indian/Hindu wedding essentials**—Underneath your mandap, your Hindu priest will normally provide several items to be placed prior to the ceremony beginning. One thing the priest will always need you to provide is a fire element. Be sure to ask your reception facility for guidelines.
- **Russian wedding essentials**—Most Russian weddings involve vodka—specifically one bottle on each table at the reception. Here, again, you will need to ask your caterer and reception facility about alcohol guidelines.

CHAPTER 6

The Savvy Social Media MOB

*I*f your daughter has access to a computer, then most likely she is spending hour after hour online finding the most splendid items for her big day. This means she is perusing blogs, pinning on Pinterest, Facebooking, Tweeting, checking out Tumblr feeds and Google+ announcements, and so much more. But computers are really becoming secondary to smartphones. If your daughter has a smartphone, she probably has access to a whole slew of other social media sites like Instagram and other amazing apps. Does this paragraph read like hieroglyphics to you? Then you must keep reading!

Using Social Media Gracefully

Social media is essentially broken up into two different categories: web-based and mobile-based sites and applications. Both help people communicate with one another. Social media is all about interactive conversations using text, photos, audio clips, and videos. For the most part, brides are finding more and more ideas for their weddings via social media platforms. As the mother of the bride, be prepared to download apps that can help you with planning your daughter's wedding. Social media apps on smartphones are quickly becoming the number-one way that brides are planning their weddings. Using social media gracefully becomes something of utmost importance when planning a wedding alongside your daughter.

Social Media on the Web

There are thousands of social media sites on the Internet. Currently the most popular sites among brides and grooms are blogs, Pinterest, Lover.ly, Tumblr, Facebook, and Twitter. Knowing what these sites are is one thing; knowing how to use them is a whole other story. Some sites are basically just informative, where users can make comments or purchases, while others set up both parties (the creator of content and the end user) for interaction.

Social Media on Smartphones

What's a smartphone? A smartphone is basically a phone that has computing capabilities similar to an actual computer. Things like music applications, Internet applications, and cameras are the most popular features you will find on a smartphone. The more capabilities a smartphone has, the "smarter" it is. Smartphones have become so popular that they are outnumbering personal computers in sales. Since people (that includes your daughter) are on the move so much, the smartphone is what keeps them informed while not being bound to a desk and chair.

 Alert

As with anything online, be sure you are careful when leaving comments on blogs. What goes on the Internet stays on the Internet. Be sure to protect your identity and sign up on the blog as anonymously as possible. You might want to consider setting up an e-mail account just for wedding-related communication to protect your identity.

Smartphones have virtual stores where the smartphone user can download applications (also called "apps") to increase the capabilities of the phone. There are distinctive mobile apps that are designed for brides and for photo sharing. These will be explored later in the chapter.

The main idea behind using social media gracefully on your smartphone is to not overshare. You need to make a plan with your daughter so you are both on the same page in regard to what you will be sharing on the web throughout the entire wedding process. You also need to consider how much you comment on other people's wedding planning processes. Everyone's wedding is different for a reason. Everyone is unique and that is why weddings are so much fun and magical.

Guest Considerations

Everyone will be coming to the wedding with cell phones in tow. Most of them will have Instagram, Facebook, and Twitter already installed on their phones. Almost every single cell phone in the world has some sort of picture-taking capabilities. When planning the wedding day, you need to keep your guests in mind when incorporating social media.

Keeping It Social

If your daughter is all about having the most social media–centered wedding on the planet, get ready to download every app she sends you. She is trying to share information with you and everyone else. Most of the time, the apps that are created with weddings in mind are all about making the wedding planning process easier and keeping guests informed.

If your daughter is opting for a blog to keep guests current or a simple website with updates about the wedding, there are apps for that. Your daughter will also probably want to create a hashtag, which will help tag everything that she is posting on the web about the wedding day. For example, if your daughter's name is Rachel and her fiancé's name is Pat, her hashtag might be "#rachelandpatgethitched." A hashtag is all about describing the big day in one word with the number sign (#) before it. Before you know it, you, the bridesmaids, the groomsmen, and a whole slew of guests will be using the hashtag as the date draws near. On the day of the wedding, you might want to have a sign somewhere letting your guests know the hashtag to use when they post photos to social media.

Wedding, Health, and Fashion Blogs

Blogs helped start the social media revolution. What's a blog? A blog is a website that is updated periodically by its author(s) or creator(s) (called "bloggers") based on its subject content. The most recent posts on the blog are always shown first, and most blogs have decent search capabilities so you can search within them for specific topics. In the world of weddings, blogs have become an amazing tool for wedding professionals to showcase their recent weddings and give advice to engaged couples. Most bloggers allow end users to leave comments on the posts—hence the "social" aspect of a blog.

Wedding Blogs

There are two different types of wedding bloggers. There are wedding professionals who "blog" (write) about their work, ideas, and advice. The other (and most widely read) wedding bloggers post items, such as submissions from their readers and wedding professionals, on their blogs and will sometimes also provide photo-shoot ideas for engaged couples. This is not actually a professional wedding service. Now, this is not to say that the folks who run these popular blogs are not wedding professionals themselves; it just means that the sites are not dedicated to selling their services. This way, they can be unbiased as to who submits to their site and can showcase anyone's work based on their niche audience. Every single wedding blog that has a large following typically has a very specific niche and specific audience. However, there are a few major wedding blogs that have their own niches but appeal to a very wide audience. Here are a few of the top wedding blogs:

- *www.stylemepretty.com*—This blog covers the widest range of weddings, and appeals to the general masses instead of a niche.
- *www.100layercake.com/blog*—This site started as just a blog, but now it allows users to shop and has a list of DIY resources and a vendor directory. This site showcases amazing details from weddings around the country as well as DIY ideas.
- *www.weddingchicks.com*—This incredibly useful blog is a real wedding and DIY mecca, complete with bouquet "recipes" and "hand-picked" vendors and recommendations.
- *www.theperfectpalette.com*—This blog is all about color inspiration for the wedding day. If your daughter has no idea what to do with the color peach, this blog can help her figure out how to mix and match color palettes.

- *www.ruffledblog.com*—An adorable blog dedicated to vintage, indie, and DIY inspiration, along with a marketplace where you can sell used weddings items.
- *www.thebudgetsavvybride.com*—This blog helps brides on any budget with planning and strategy as well as DIY items and giveaways. A must-read for every mother of the bride!
- *www.oncewed.com*—A blog dedicated to designer weddings for less. Its creator, Emily Newman, was the first blogger to provide space on her blog for selling used wedding dresses. It also has its own print magazine.
- *www.junebugweddings.com*—A blog known for its incredible photography and wedding planning resources for high-end weddings.
- *www.thebrokeassbride.com*—Excuse the language and love the blogger! Dana LaRue was inspired to write her blog after working with a small budget for her first wedding. Her blog is the number-one blog for brides on a budget.
- *www.eco-beautifulweddings.com*—This blog is all about creating eco-friendly weddings that are still stylish. It is the first blog to publish both an online and print magazine all about eco-friendly weddings.
- *www.groomsadvice.com*—The absolute best blog on the Internet for grooms. It provides help with bachelor parties, toasts, best-man duties, and much more!
- *www.perfectboundblog.com*—This fashionista blog is all about dressing up the wedding party the right way. Lots of gowns to dream about on it!

- *www.thesweetestoccasion.com*—This blog is chock-full of incredible design elements for any occasion. Lots of ideas about paper, décor, and desserts!
- *www.iloveswmag.com*—This blog is an amazing accompaniment to *Southern Weddings* magazine. Brides love the personalities of the editors and all the wedding ideas with Southern charm and hospitality.
- *www.brendasweddingblog.com*—One of the most extensive and informative wedding blogs, with ideas for everything from favors to cakes, along with constant giveaways! A daily must-read.
- *www.everylastdetailblog.com*—A beautiful and fresh blog with detailed posts and gorgeous real weddings as well as great advice from a real wedding professional.
- *www.elizabethannedesigns.com*—One of the very first wedding blogs that dedicated itself to tabletop ideas, DIY inspiration, real weddings, and an incredible curated vendor directory.
- *www.eleganceandsimplicity.com/blog*—A blog all about wedding planning, going green, wedding style, and mother-of-the-bride hints!

Health Blogs

Weddings are pretty much the one time in most brides' lives that they will go nuts over losing weight and staying healthy for the big day. The following are the best blogs that brides (and grooms) can use to help them get fit and stay healthy both before and after the wedding day. Who's to say you won't learn a few things yourself—you have to get into a pretty dress, too!

- *www.shape.com*—*Shape* magazine has a whole section of its website dedicated to fitness tips and advice for getting in shape for the big day.
- *www.fitnessmagazine.com*—Another popular magazine featuring specific workouts to tone different parts of the body in a healthy way.
- *www.fitbottomedgirls.com*—This site provides workout and food options for women of all shapes and sizes. Its motto is "Keeping a lid on the junk in the trunk."
- *www.crankyfitness.com*—This blog is funny yet super helpful when it comes to staying healthy. A great daily read.
- *www.fitnessista.com*—A blog dedicated to food that is good for you and general fitness points.

 Question

What if you want to find more information on local vendors and ideas?

The best thing to do, if you live in a large metropolitan area, is to do a simple Google search: your city + blog. This way, you can find a localized blog that can really show you amazing examples from your hometown!

Fashion Blogs

Gone are the days when brides were looking for inspiration for weddings from only wedding websites and blogs. Brides want to make sure their wedding stands out and is a little different from those that have come before them. For example, brides want fabulous and different shoes for their weddings (no more white wedding shoes!). The best place to find such inspiration is daily fashion blogs. Here are a few popular ones:

- *www.fashionista.com*—Here you can find out about all the latest buzz in the fashion world. From Fashion Weeks (in New York, London, Milan, and Paris) to celebrities (and what they are wearing at parties), you will be engulfed in the magic of the fashion industry. There are also great shopping and photo features.
- *www.whowhatwear.com*—A beautiful and edgy fashion blog focused on celebrities and trendsetters around the word. There is also a great section called "Ask a Stylist," and shopping, too!
- *www.theglamourai.com*—This blog has nothing but amazingly beautiful photos for endless inspiration. The blog features outfit inspiration, fashion, home décor, beauty, and shopping.
- *www.becauseimaddicted.net*—A blog dedicated to fashion, music, food, and art. Based in Los Angeles, this blog showcases some of the cutest, youngest, and freshest posts on the latest fashion trends.

There really are so many blogs that can provide inspiration to both you and your daughter. Taking a look at them should make gathering ideas easier for you.

Pinterest

Pinterest (*www.pinterest.com*) is one of the largest social media networks, and it looks and feels like it was created just for weddings (but it wasn't)! Since you and your daughter will undoubtedly want to see ideas and organize them in one place, Pinterest can be a big help.

How to Use Pinterest

The basic concept of Pinterest is "pinning" photos to boards that you create. Pinterest is actually one of the easier social media sites to join. Just enter your e-mail address and you'll be up and running in no time. Once you are on the site, you will see all sorts of photos. To view wedding-related photos, find the drop-down menu at the top of the page and select the "Weddings" category (located under "Everything"). Here you will see a stream of photos of wedding ideas that you can start pinning to boards. Click on a photo, and once your mouse is hovering over the photo, click on the button that says "Repin." At this point, a small box will pop up and prompt you to start creating "boards" to categorize your pins. So if you see a photo of a cute cake, call your board "Wedding Cakes" and then write a little description (or keep the one that is already in the box below) and hit "Pin It." Then, whenever you see another cake you like, you can pin it to the same board. Repeat the same process for other categories or just create one board for all of your wedding ideas until you master the world of Pinterest!

Another way to pin items to your boards is directly from another website (like a blog). At the top of the main Pinterest page, go to the "About" drop-down menu and click on the "Pin It" button. Here you will find instructions on how to add this function to your browser so you can pin items onto your boards whenever you see anything you or your daughter might like for the wedding. You can also upload a photo from your computer by clicking on the "Add +" button at the top of the page. You can also just "like" a pin if you don't want to create a board for it.

These are literally just the basics of how Pinterest works. Be careful, though; once you get on the site, you might get addicted to it (as there are all sorts of other categories to make boards for)! Pinterest also has an app where you can pin away on your smartphone!

You can also create a secret board for you and your daughter to pin things that only the two of you have access to. When creating the board, there is a simple option to indicate whether or not you want it to be secret. It also gives you the option to invite others to pin to the secret board. For example, you might want to include the bridesmaids or the mother of the groom.

Similar Photo-Centric Sites

Pinterest is the inspiration for many other hybrid sites, but there are two sites in particular that have a Pinterest-like feel to them just for wedding inspiration: *www.lover.ly* and *www.weddinggawker.com*.

- *www.lover.ly*—Yes, you type that into your browser exactly as it is written here: "lover dot ly." No need to include "www," but if you do, you will still end up on Lover.ly. This site is set up similarly to Pinterest, but it has a shopping function and it basically pulls photos only from blogs that are affiliated with the site. Wedding blogs sign up (or get approached by the site) to have their photos feed into the site. Brides and grooms log on to "bundle" photos together (the same thing as "pinning," basically) to create boards of wedding inspiration. The site is truly lovely to browse, as you can search by color, which is perfect for weddings. The site tends to showcase mostly midlevel to high-end weddings.
- *www.weddinggawker.com*—Weddinggawker has a similar vibe to Lover.ly in the sense that it just showcases wedding photos. However, it showcases more types of wedding ideas, and it helps you tag photos so you can take notes on each photo. You can then share the photos with your friends. The site also has a great search function. In addition, you can very easily post a photo from the website onto Pinterest, Facebook, Twitter, and other social media platforms.

Facebook

Facebook (*www.facebook.com*) is one of the largest social media sites in the history of the web. Facebook is all about sharing ideas, photos, and videos with your "friends." Friends can be your actual friends and family, or they can be associates, businesses, or people who just want to know what you are up to.

Facebook for the Wedding Day and Beyond

The idea behind using Facebook for wedding planning is to share ideas with your network of friends online. If you already have a Facebook page, you know that you can just post questions about the wedding, and then your friends can give you advice by commenting on your timeline. This is especially helpful if you live far away from friends and family and want to keep them informed about the wedding day. But don't post too much information about the wedding, as you don't want to give away the surprise element for your guests.

Alert

While Facebook is a powerful tool, it also can really diminish your privacy if you post too much about yourself. Be sure to read through their privacy and security sections should you sign up for Facebook to help share ideas for the wedding day.

Another way to use Facebook for wedding planning is to "tag" people in photos that you post to your page in order to encourage them to provide input and ideas. Also, after the wedding is over, Facebook is the perfect place to post photos so others can see what a beautiful day it was without clogging up their e-mail inboxes with images!

If you don't have a Facebook account, don't worry; it is really easy to sign up. You can also enlist your daughter's help with how to become "friends" with her online. Facebook gives you the ability to set up a secret group, where just those who are involved in the wedding party can share ideas. You or your daughter can be the administrator (admin) of the secret page and invite the wedding party and others to visit the page to post ideas as well (without the rest of the world being able to see).

Facebook is also available on most smartphones, making it easy to take photos and make comments or ask questions and post them directly to Facebook right from your phone.

The best feature of Facebook is the ability to connect with old and new friends online. Who knows, you may find an old classmate who is throwing a wedding for her daughter, too!

Instagram

Instagram (*www.instagram.com*) is one of the most popular apps for smartphones. However, it is different from any other social media platform in that it focuses on the photo-sharing aspect of social media. Until recently, the only people who could use Instagram were iPhone and Android smartphone users. However, since Facebook purchased Instagram, it has become the easiest way to post photos on multiple platforms, such as Facebook, Twitter, Tumblr, Flickr, and Foursquare.

Instagram and Wedding Planning

Like Pinterest, Instagram is truly one of the most addictive social media platforms. However, Instagram is more popular for capturing and sharing photos in your daily life and commenting on them, functioning almost like a daily photo journal. People can follow you and comment on your posts. You can also follow people and make comments on their posts. This platform is great for when your daughter or you are shopping and visiting vendors. You can take a quick photo with your smartphone and post it immediately to Instagram.

Instagram is also really fun in the sense that it has a wide array of filters to make your photos look more professional. One of the best ways to find useful wedding information on Instagram is by using hashtags. You can use hashtags to search for photos (of certain types of dresses or flowers, for example) and local vendors through the search function. You will find tons of photos from local florists on Instagram who use hashtags to describe their photos (for example, #dcflorist if you live in Washington, DC). These hashtags help MOBs like you find that perfect bridal bouquet and more.

Twitter

Twitter (*www.twitter.com*) is a social media network that enables you to write questions or statements in 140 characters or fewer (known as "Tweets") and send them out to other users. Your Tweets will then show up in your Twitter feed. Your "followers" (those Twitter members who are following you) can either respond by "Retweeting" what you posted or just answering, like a text message.

Tweeting for the Wedding Day

Twitter is also great for wedding planning because of its search feature. Many companies (large and small) will post giveaways and discounts on their Twitter feeds. Twitter also makes it extremely easy to interact with vendors. You can follow a person or a company by going to their Twitter page and pressing the "Follow" button. Once you do this, you can find out who is Tweeting with you by clicking on the "Connect" button at the top of your Twitter page. If you mention another person on Twitter by his Twitter "handle" (which is his name on Twitter), it will show up in his "Mentions" stream and he will see what has been said about him. Twitter also allows you to share images. As with most social media sites, Twitter is also available on smartphones.

Tumblr

No, *Tumblr* is not a misspelling! It's an actual website where users can easily follow blog authors either from their computers or on their smartphones. In short, it is a network of thousands of blogs, and users can view all the blogs they want in one single stream, or one long webpage. Additionally, it is also a great platform for bloggers who love to update their blogs via their smartphones with photos and videos.

Using Tumblr for Weddings

First, you need to sign up for an account at *www .tumblr.com*. Once you have an account, you can follow all of your favorite Tumblr bloggers in one stream. The best way to use Tumblr for wedding planning is to do a simple search. Search for a topic, and when you find subjects and photos you like, click on the button in the upper-right corner that says "Follow." This way, every time you log into Tumblr, their photos and blog entries will show up in your blog stream.

Tumblr is great for wedding planning because it allows you and your daughter to share an account to post photos about wedding ideas. This can be used to create a journal about the process, which is a fun way to bond and document your time planning together. This might be a great way to keep records for your next daughter's wedding, or for the bride to show her children one day!

Google+

If you've ever done an Internet search, you've heard of Google (this is where the term *googling* came from). The same company has created a social media site called Google+, which is similar to Facebook. Google+ users can provide updates about what they are doing and where they are doing it via their computers or cell phones. What sets this application apart from Facebook is its use of a video-chat feature.

How to Use Google+ for the Big Day

To use Google+, you have to sign up for an account. If you have a Gmail account, they make it super easy for you to just add this platform to your existing account. If you do not have a Gmail account, you can sign up with another e-mail account (such as Yahoo! or Hotmail). Once you've created your Google+ account, you can post questions and statements along with photos. You can separate what you would like to post through a system called "circles," and whenever you add someone to your list of friends, you determine which circle that person belongs to. In addition, you get to create the circles. This means you can have one circle for bridesmaids, one for groomsmen, and so on. Each time you post something, you can either make it available to everyone you are connected to or just to certain circles. The circle capability, and the privacy it provides, is one big difference between Google+ and Facebook.

In essence, Google+ works just like Facebook, but it is cumbersome to use in comparison to Facebook, so most people are not using Google+ to its full capacity just yet.

Wedding Apps for the Big Day

There is no way to list all of the apps available to help you plan for your daughter's wedding day. In addition to the major social media sites that have their own apps mentioned in this chapter, here is a list of the most widely used and most popular.

- **Paperless Post**—This app is an accompaniment to the website *www.paperlesspost.com*. Paperless Post is one of the most widely used online invitation apps for weddings. You can use the app to track who has opened electronic Save the Date cards and invitations. Their invitations can be used for engagement parties, bridal showers, rehearsal dinners, and the wedding day (and really any event that requires an invitation). The app lets you track RSVPs and send messages to guests right from your smartphone.
- **Yapp**—This is a great app for families and bridal parties to use. It is like having a private message board for just the people in your wedding party. Yapp (*www.yapp.us*) is particularly useful for families and wedding parties that include people in different countries.
- **WeddingWire**—WeddingWire (*www.weddingwire.com*) is one of the easiest websites for couples to use for wedding planning and seeing reviews of local vendors. It really leads the wedding industry in technology and educating brides and grooms. The app is interactive and helpful for the wedding planning basics.
- **Evernote**—Evernote (*https://evernote.com*) is one of the most useful tools in the app world in general. This app is all about keeping your to-do lists, notes, and ideas organized. It also allows you to share your notes with others. Another great feature for Type A brides and MOBs is the ability to check things off as you go.
- **Appy Couple**—This app (*www.appycouple.com*) is all about consolidating everything about your daughter's wedding day into one place. There is a small fee for

making your life so easy. Everything from photo sharing to RSVP services is included!

"Unplugged" Weddings

Many couples are just not interested in posting everything about their weddings on the Internet. When it comes to small children, this is especially true. While it might be cute that the flower girl went screaming down the aisle half-naked, having that on Facebook is not a good idea. If the couple does not want social media to be the center of attention for the ceremony or reception, be sure to communicate that to your guests. During the ceremony, there is nothing more annoying than seeing thirty guests lift up their tablets and smartphones to take pictures. The devices get in the way of other guests, and it is really just downright rude. The ceremony is the reason why everyone is there for the wedding day, and it is a momentous social rite for anyone getting married. The seriousness of a wedding ceremony is the number-one reason why you have a photographer and videographer to capture the moments in the best possible way. You can ask your guests to silence their phones for the ceremony in writing on a sign or in the program. Your officiant can also make the announcement at the beginning of the ceremony.

CHAPTER 7

Let the (Other) Parties Begin!

*M*ost brides find themselves in the guest-of-honor seat at several parties in the months leading up to the big event. What are your duties as far as these soirees are concerned? It depends on how involved you want to be, how involved the hostess of the party wants you to be, and the party itself. This chapter will give you the skinny on some of the pre-wedding parties you might be involved with—in one way or another.

Party-Planning Basics

Once your daughter becomes engaged, there will be parties galore. While in some cases the only thing you will be responsible for is showing up with your best MOB smile, in some instances you will be involved with much of the planning. In fact, the pre-wedding parties are where you might gain party-planning insight and learn valuable research skills that you can carry over into planning the wedding itself. This all depends, of course, on how large and/or formal each event will be. If you're thinking about hosting an at-home engagement party, for example, you'll have to either find a caterer or come up with a mathematical equation to figure out how many gallons of macaroni salad and how many packages of rolls you'll need for fifty hungry guests. These particular planning skills may or may not come in handy for planning the reception.

 Alert

Don't go way over your budget when planning a party. It's very easy to start overspending once you're presented with the most magnificent options. Stick to your plan, and don't allow yourself to be pulled into anything that you might regret later. (Remember, you're going to be shelling out for a wedding soon.)

File It under *Organized*

An organizational system, whether that means colored folders, computer files, and/or an actual file cabinet, will be your best friend when you're putting together an event like this. Organization is the key to successful party planning. You'll never attend a creative, brilliantly planned party and hear the hostess say, "You know, it just all took care of itself. I don't even remember the name of the caterer." (If she does say this, she's not telling the truth.)

If disorganization has been a lifelong problem for you, you're probably thinking that there's no hope—disorder is order for you, and you can't change now. Wrong, Mom. There's always hope for even the most die-hard clutter lovers. How does one get organized quickly and painlessly, you ask?

- **Start small.** Don't try to compartmentalize your entire life at once. Planning an event is a nice way to segue into overall organization.
- **Invest in supplies.** Getting things in order doesn't have to be expensive. Buy a used file cabinet, pick up a box of file folders, or install some organizational software on your PC. The money you spend will be well worth the aggravation you save yourself in the end.
- **Label everything.** Have one folder for receipts, another for literature on vendors, another for the guest list, etc. Put a big label on each file so that you don't accidentally lose your guest list in the recipe file.
- **Don't compare yourself to others.** Your best friend might be the most organized person on the planet; however, the system that works for her may not work for you, so go into this with an open mind. Find your own best methods for keeping information tidy.

A positive attitude is required for those who are striving for order. Do your best to stay on top of things. (Don't let papers pile up until you have to sort them into their various files—something's sure to get lost in the shuffle.) You might surprise yourself, and you might discover that you enjoy being able to find what you're looking for when you're looking for it (and not three months later).

Be Strong!

Depending on the size of the party, you may find yourself interviewing various vendors. If you've never been in this position before, and you're not comfortable asking difficult (or even necessary) questions, you might feel a little shy or awkward about the whole thing. Remember this: Vendors deal with potential customers every single day. These customers ask the most off-the-wall, outrageous, beside-the-point questions. They've cleared the path for you already. There is absolutely nothing you can ask a vendor that she hasn't already been asked. So don't be bashful.

Don't let a banquet manager, restaurant owner, or caterer allow you to feel less than intelligent. While it's true that certain businesses make their living from weddings and pre-wedding parties (and therefore know a lot about them—more than the average bride or MOB), part of their job is (nicely) providing you with all the information you're looking for so that you aren't entering into a blind deal with them. Many wedding-related businesses are excellent in the area of dealing with potential clients; these people know that alienating customers is not in their best interest. It's up to you to have a list of questions and to ask them. As nice as these vendors may be, they aren't usually known for their clairvoyance.

 Essential

When interviewing vendors, remember you're potentially entering into a business deal. That means *you're* paying *them* to provide *you* with a service. Any vendor who isn't willing or able to adequately address your questions and/ or concerns is not someone you want to do business with.

Stick to the Plan

Though it's easy to become distracted by the beauty of banquet rooms and the creativity of various caterers, when you're looking for the best vendor(s) for the party you're planning, keep in mind that you do have a budget to work with. Yes, the room may be lovely, but what about its price? The menu sounds scrumptious, but is it what you were thinking of in the first place? Keep your guard up just enough to retain a clear picture of the party you were planning before you stepped into the caterer's (or banquet manager's) office and seated yourself in the plush side chair.

Stifle Those Comments, Mom

Pretend you're hosting a party. It can be a birthday party, a cocktail party, a dinner party—choose an event. You've booked a restaurant, you've chosen a menu, perhaps you've even researched some icebreaker games. Your plans are working out well until you receive a call from one of your invited guests who tells you that you're doing it all wrong. The location stinks, you should be feeding the guests more than finger foods and cake, and don't even get her going on the topic of the games (she thinks they're tasteless). What would you do? Give her a piece of your mind? Disinvite her?

Now pretend that your daughter's friends or in-laws are planning a pre-wedding party for her and you're displeased with the location, the menu, and the activities. What are you going to do now? The right answer: you're going to show up and be a gracious guest.

Alert

Being the MOB doesn't mean you're allowed to criticize with impunity. Though you may be very unhappy with the way another hostess handled your daughter's engagement party or shower, hold your tongue. There's no way you can chastise a hostess and come away looking like a decent human.

It's wrong for an invited guest (you, in this instance) to criticize a party. It's worse than wrong—it's rude and crass (two words that should never be associated with the MOB). Bottom line: if you're planning a party, you're free to go in any direction you want with it—just remember that every other hostess holds that same privilege. It would be bad enough for the bride to complain about a party that's given in her honor; it's ten times worse for you to stick your nose into the matter, proclaiming that your little girl deserves better.

If your inquiries and comments are your way of saying, "I want to help," try to find a better way to phrase it, such as coming right out and offering to be of assistance to the party planner. If she needs your help, she'll call on you, and if she doesn't, you'll just have to take your seat along with all of the other guests. Even though you are the MOB, you can't force a hostess to accept your help.

Decisions for Pre-Wedding Parties

The bride's attendants are traditionally expected to host a shower for her. If the wedding is only months away and there's been no mention of a party, go ahead and give them a little nudge—or plan it yourself. (Though etiquette states that the bride's mom should not host her shower, it's more common these days for people to toss etiquette and do what's easiest and most convenient.) If the bridesmaids have everything under control, you may be asked to provide them with a guest list.

Should the bride's friends invite you to her bachelorette party, you may want to think twice about attending—depending on how you feel about wild behavior. Most bachelorette parties entail a lot of drinking, references to the male anatomy, and maybe a male stripper or two. If this sounds like your idea of a good time, count yourself in. If not, skip it.

Bridal Shower

In many wedding etiquette books, you'll learn that the MOB is supposed to "keep her nose out" of the bridal-shower planning. Occasionally, however, especially in the case of the younger bride (and her college-aged bridesmaids), the shower can end up being the least fantastic event for your daughter if no one has any idea how to plan one. Are you allowed to save the day?

Get the Planning Started

Younger bridesmaids (or those who haven't read etiquette books) may not have any clue that they're supposed to plan a shower for their friend. If the maid of honor has not done anything about the shower, a quick e-mail from you asking what the date of the shower is going to be is usually enough to get the ball rolling. The maid of honor is typically supposed to take charge of this particular event. Of course, when you send the e-mail, you can always offer your help if she needs it. You'll be able to gauge from her response whether a party is in the works or if this is the first she's heard or thought of it.

 Essential

Since showers are ideally held about two months prior to the wedding, you'll want to know the game plan at least four months before the ceremony. That way, if the bridesmaids *are* delinquent in their responsibilities, you can step in and whip up something yourself.

Something else to consider: has your daughter stood up in any of her bridesmaids' weddings? Did she contribute to the planning and the cost of their showers? If not, you can be sure that at least one of the bridesmaids is wondering why she's being held responsible for the very same duty your daughter neglected during her engagement.

Mom to the Rescue

If the bridesmaids have neglected their duties, you don't need to list their names as hostesses on the shower invitations. Since many MOBs do host bridal showers these days, go ahead and put your own name on that line, or choose another relative or friend to be the figurehead for the day.

Are you entitled to demand a financial contribution from the bridesmaids for a shower that you're planning? Not really. Even though the girls should have made the plans themselves, you can't insist that they pitch in on particulars that were completely of your choosing. The place you've chosen might be out of their price range— and they may have hesitated with the planning in the first place because they're all broke. You can certainly request that they pitch in on the party, but you can't place liens on their bank accounts if they fail to do so.

If you decide to take the reins of planning this event, or at least want to help organize it, you'll need to know what showers are like these days, and how to make your daughter's both memorable and enjoyable. The following sections will give you some planning pointers.

Dish It Out

What will you feed the ladies who attend the shower? Most often, showers are afternoon events and include lunch or a high tea of sorts. Just be aware that most guests will expect to eat something substantial, and since the vast majority of them will be lugging a gift for the bride along with them, you want to make sure they feel welcome and well taken care of for the afternoon.

A shower can be held at a special venue or restaurant. One of the most common places to hold a bridal shower is in someone's home. If you're inviting seventy-five women, really consider whether you're up to the task of setting up tables and chairs and cooking for such a large group. It's definitely easier on your back to hold a large party in a restaurant or the local art gallery. If you're renting chairs, tables, linens, and a tent (and glasses . . . and silverware) for a backyard party, it might be less expensive to just move the party elsewhere. If you have loads of helpers, though, as well as plenty of room and folding tables stored in your basement, a party at home might be a viable option.

For a large, at-home party, you might want to look into hiring a caterer, unless you and your family love the idea of cooking for the masses. Just make sure before you commit to all of this work that your assistants are as committed as you are. You're amazing all right, but you are one woman with one set of hands. You can't do everything.

You'll need to make sure the ladies have plenty to drink. If you're offering wine and cocktails to your guests, make sure they're given a choice of nonalcoholic drinks as well. If you're hosting a party at home, make sure you've stocked the bar with lemons, limes, celery, olives, stirrers—any finishing touches that your guests will need for their drinks.

 Alert

Don't forget about dessert! Wherever ladies gather to celebrate an upcoming wedding, it's only natural that someone will be looking for sweets. Shower cakes are traditional in some parts of the country, while in other areas, anything goes—and usually goes fast!

Play Along

There are two schools of thought on shower games: Ladies either love 'em or hate 'em. There's no middle ground. Regardless of your personal feelings, take a look at your guest list and ask yourself which guests will be expecting to compete with the other ladies for a prize. Like it or not, members of the older generation (and even some members of the younger generations) might well be expecting to play a game or two—that's what ladies do at showers, as far as they're concerned.

There are some safe standards that almost every guest will tolerate (such as "Guess How Many Heart Candies Are in the Jar"), and then there are games that might only serve to divide your guests into two camps: those who will play, and those who won't. (The opposing groups will eye each other suspiciously for the rest of the after-noon.) These are usually group activities (for example, something along the lines of each table being forced to compose a single poem about the bride and groom). If the guests don't know each other extremely well, your well-intentioned attempt at trying to make them get to know each other could backfire. Unless you and the bride really, really love shower games, try to keep them simple and as humiliation-free for the guests as possible.

We Have a Winner!

Offer prizes for the winners and favors (or door prizes) for all of your guests, and have plenty on hand in case there's a dispute and you end up with double or triple winners somewhere along the line. When you're purchasing these items, think about buying something either perishable or practical—and avoid choosing prizes that will end up in someone's junk drawer or in the trash. Ideas for favors and prizes include popular gel soaps and perfumes; small houseplants and succulents; candy and chocolates; local goods like jams, jellies, and apples from the local farmer; and gift certificates.

 Fact

Coed showers are gaining in popularity. This is a nice idea for a couple of reasons: A coed shower gets everyone together before the wedding, and the couple may receive some practical items (such as tools) that rarely find their way onto a bridal registry.

There are many, many other options and ideas for games and prizes. One last word of caution, though: think twice before you personalize these items with the bride and/or groom's names. Your guests are more likely to use (and appreciate) something that they feel is theirs—and they won't if your daughter's name is all over those otherwise lovely little notepads and frames you've purchased as door prizes.

Theme Showers

Who doesn't love a good theme party? The possibilities for shower themes are endless, because a bride-to-be usually needs just about everything for her new home and her new life. Some guests really love theme parties, because they know what they're shopping for—it actually might make their work a little easier. Consider these gift-giving themes:

- Kitchen
- Lingerie
- Stock the bar
- Recipe or cooking exchange

The guests can get as creative as they want, and the bride will end up with a house full of useful supplies.

Theme showers can take off in any direction. If the newlyweds will be entertaining frequently in their new home, a stock-the-bar shower might be a great idea for them: Each guest brings a bottle for the newlyweds' liquor cabinet. (Any couple who has ever had to stock their own bar knows that this expense adds up quickly, especially if you're starting from scratch.)

Bridesmaids' Luncheon

Technically, the bride is supposed to take charge of this gathering; however, since you're supposed to be helping the bride, you might find yourself lending a hand. The bridesmaids' luncheon is strictly optional. If several of the bridesmaids are coming from out of town, and there's no way to coordinate everyone's schedules before the day of the wedding (or rehearsal), it's probably best to just skip it. Trying to squeeze in a luncheon on the day of the ceremony will defeat the purpose of this gathering. It's supposed to be a nice, relaxing afternoon for the bride and her girlfriends.

 Essential

This get-together doesn't have to be lunch. The bride can turn it into a bridesmaids' dinner, a night on the town, a day at the spa, or a movie marathon night at the bride's home.

Since this is a thank-you from the bride to her attendants, each one should be included. Some brides also invite the moms (and if you're invited, the groom's mom really should be, too), and, depending on the time and location of the get-together, some may invite the flower girl (whose mother should also be in attendance). This is an intimate get-together, so the guest list shouldn't read like a phone book.

Saying Thanks

The bridesmaids' luncheon is the bride's way of showing her appreciation for the hard work her bridesmaids have done. This event is a great time for the bride to give her attendants the gifts she's chosen for them. At the very least, bridesmaids have spent quite a bit of money on their ensembles for the wedding, but they also should have paid for the shower, a shower and wedding gift for the bride, and their personal travel expenses, if any. That's a lot to ask from a girlfriend, and even though the attendants knew what they were getting into when they accepted a role in the wedding party, they'll appreciate your daughter's acknowledgment of their efforts.

On the other hand, a bride will occasionally find herself saddled with unruly and unpleasant bridesmaids who are bound and determined to give her nothing but grief. In this case, should she still thank them by hosting a lunch in their honor? Let common sense prevail.

Fun Ideas for Treating the Bridesmaids

Does your daughter need some ideas to make this luncheon interesting and unique? Don't be tied to having just a simple luncheon! Here are a few ideas:

- **For the "traditional" bridesmaid**—A tradition widely practiced in the South includes presenting a cake at the luncheon with some symbolic meaning baked in. In one variation, the bridesmaids dig into a pink cake that includes some sort of trinket—a coin, a ring, or a thimble. The lucky lady who finds the trinket in her slice of cake is the next to walk down the aisle. Another variation on the cake comes from Victorian England. The cake is placed on top of charms, which are attached to ribbons that are long enough to hang off the cake plate. Each bridesmaid pulls a ribbon to reveal her charm at the other end. The bride can choose the charms herself (available where wedding supplies are sold) and attach meaning to them in her own creative way.

- **For the "cosmopolitan" clique**—A bridesmaids' luncheon can also be high tea at one of her favorite hotels (think the Ritz-Carlton!). Nothing is more cosmopolitan and swanky than having high tea with petit fours and mini sandwiches to gab over!
- **For "girly-girl" bridesmaids**—A girls' day out at the spa is perfect. Nothing says "girlie girl" more than having your manicures, pedicures, and facials done at a private spa! Be sure to arrange for healthy food in between spa services. This is something you can do the day before the wedding to make sure all their pretty nails are ready for the big day!
- **For the "sporty" bridesmaids**—Depending on the time of year, a fun night out with the girls at a sporting event followed by guacamole and chips at the local Mexican restaurant might be right up her alley.

Keep in mind that it does not have to be a luncheon! You know your little girl's personality the best! So make suggestions based on her personality. While she might be treating the bridesmaids to a big date, you want to make sure she enjoys herself, too!

Bachelorette Party

Yes, the bride gets to have her one night to go crazy prior to the wedding. No, it does not have to be a trip to the male-strip club (especially if she begs you to stop that from happening). It can be a girls' night out at any bar, restaurant, or club, or a relaxed evening at home watching her favorite movies. Whatever the maid of honor (or you) has planned for her, it should be something that she will like and enjoy remembering!

Welcome Reception and Rehearsal

When it comes to large weddings, especially ones that have a large number of out-of-town guests, you may want to consider having a welcome reception. Some brides and grooms like to combine the welcome reception with the rehearsal. However, if many of your guests are coming on a Thursday (which is the case with many destination weddings), a small welcome reception with light refreshments is always a wonderful thought. Guests from out of town will be coming to the various hotels at various hours, and the welcome reception is a way to get them situated in the new city they are in. This is a great time to tell them about local favorite restaurants and interesting sightseeing tours. The rehearsal dinner can also be used for this.

Post-Wedding Reception

A relatively new concept that is gaining popularity is the post-wedding reception. This get-together is typically informal. This is a gathering place for all of the wedding guests who still want to party once the reception ends. A popular place for the post-wedding reception is a local bar or even the bar in the hotel where the majority of the guests are staying. Typically, this event does not require a budget and guests are responsible for paying for their own drinks and snacks. However, if you have room in your budget, booking a fun place for guests who want to extend the party will always be welcomed. Think cocktails and snack food, and you have yourself a post-wedding reception!

Brunch

The post-wedding brunch is typically held the day after the wedding and gives the wedding party and the guests more time to say goodbye and chat about the wedding day. Many will be on their way to the airport and will appreciate having something to eat before they leave.

 Fact

It's your prerogative to host a post-wedding brunch, but you're not required to do so. If you do choose to honor the newly married couple with another party, be sure to extend invitations to all of the wedding guests, but remember, not all will be able to attend.

A brunch can be held anywhere, from the hotel where the reception took place to a local restaurant to your own home. Holding a brunch at your home will help to control costs, and holding it at the hotel where the majority of the guests are staying could be a thoughtful (and more convenient) gesture.

Speech Hints and Tips

Hosts or hostesses of pre-wedding parties are often called upon to offer up some kind words regarding the engagement. The bride's dad may jump at this idea, or you may be the one who has a thing or two to say. But what *should* you say?

If you don't speak in public on a regular basis, and if the thought of holding the attention of a roomful of people makes you nervous, you might give up on the idea of offering a toast before you've given it enough thought. This is your daughter's engagement, after all, and guests will be looking to you, especially if you're the hostess, to lend your official seal of approval to the union.

If you decide to voice your endorsement, plan what you want to say. It's incredibly painful for guests to watch a speaker who's trying—and failing—to hold the floor. Give yourself plenty of time to jot down your ideas and to express them appropriately. Practice at least once, and yes, do it in front of the mirror. You want to get a feel for your facial expressions as well. If you keep it short and simple, you're sure to make the best impression.

CHAPTER 8

Dressing the Part

So much to consider! You'll need to figure out what to wear to the pre-wedding parties (which is not always as easy as it should be), and you'll have to make sure your husband isn't attempting to break out his tux from prom. The bride is begging you to help her find her ensemble; meanwhile, the bridesmaids are in a tizzy over the dress your daughter has chosen for them. It's just part of the territory for the MOB.

Simple Rules for Yourself

If you're starting to feel as though there are no longer any hard and fast rules to stick to as far as weddings and pre-wedding events are concerned, you're not far off the mark. If you're a woman who craves order and needs instructions (as specific as possible, please) in order to feel comfortable in these situations, you might be feeling a little unsure of yourself. Don't sweat it. There's very little chance that you'll show up to a wedding event dressed inappropriately . . . as long as you stick to a certain set of rules.

Rule One: Dress in Layers

As far as the pre-wedding parties are concerned, you may have no idea what you're walking into. Is a party on the patio of the tennis club a formal event or an informal one? Does a dinner at the groom's parents' house call for shorts or a dress? You can always call the host and ask, which is often the easiest and most obvious way to alleviate your fears, but if you're just not comfortable making that call, you can still show up dressed correctly and pretend you knew all along what everyone else would be wearing.

The secret? No, it's not throwing an outfit for every occasion in the trunk of your car. The trick is as simple as layering. Not sure if this is a semicasual or semidressy event? Choose a nice dress or a semidressy pair of pants, throw a nice jacket on top of it, and voilà! You're dressed for both parties. Remove the jacket if the party is more on the casual side.

 Question

What type of dress should a mother of the bride avoid?
Stay away from any dress in a neon color or animal print, a dress that shows an awful lot of cleavage, or a dress that shows your great thighs in their entirety. This goes for the wedding and any pre-wedding parties.

Rule Two: Read the Invitation

Of course, any party that is really formal will say so on the invitation. White tie (also sometimes called "ultra-formal") is the dressiest of all events and requires a full-length gown for women. Men should wear a tux with a white tie, vest, and shirt. Black tie ("formal") gives you more choices—you can wear a long dress, a cocktail dress, or separates that are dressy enough for the occasion. Men are expected to wear tuxedos. Of course, not every invitation will be so easily deciphered. What does "creative black tie" mean? And how about "black tie optional"? Are these people just out to confuse and frustrate you? If they are, they'll fail because you can refer to this handy list of dress definitions:

- **Cocktail attire:** You'll wear an elegant dress on the shorter side (knee length or just below). Men wear suits.

- **Dress casual:** Think business casual on a more formal scale.
- **Black tie optional/black tie invited:** Same as black tie (for women, at least). Men can wear tuxes or dark suits.
- **Creative black tie:** Just what it sounds like—an event that gives men and women room to experiment with newer dressy looks. (Men are limited to stylish tuxes.)

Follow your instincts (and your glossary), and you'll show up looking fabulous.

Rule Three: Keep Tabs on Your Spouse

As if dressing yourself isn't hard enough, there's your husband attempting to shimmy his way into a suit he hasn't worn in ten years. Before your hair turns white from the shock of such a sight, have a little talk with him. If he has never had a clue as to how to dress himself, help him. You can't show up looking like a movie star being accompanied by a specimen who is apparently trapped in some sort of time warp that also shrank his clothes.

Yes, some dads are eccentric, and yes, everyone may be aware that the bride's dad is known for his fashion missteps (or, more correctly, his rather intellectual disdain for fashion), but for any wedding-related event, he should look his best and be dressed appropriately.

Rule Four: Don't Upstage the Bride, Ever

MOBs often find themselves torn between wearing an absolutely smashing dress that comes very close to calling a lot of attention to them (which, of course, is what this particular dress is all about) and respecting the rule that states that the bride should be the prettiest woman at the wedding. Is it right that you should be condemned to don a lesser frock just so that your daughter won't be upset?

Know that you shouldn't outdo the bride on her wedding day or at any of her pre-wedding parties. Yes, you look great in that dress you're dying to wear, but you'll look just as good in something more subdued (even if you hate and regularly rebel against that word).

The Perfect Dress—Where Is It?

Some women love shopping; others abhor it. If you fall into the former group, finding a dress for the wedding will be a piece of cake (or at least you'll have a blast looking); if you fall into the latter group, you may be putting off this task until the very last minute.

Start Early

Dresses for weddings (including the bride's dress, the attendants' dresses, and the dresses for the moms) don't change too drastically from one year to the next. You'll want something that's appropriate for the time of year. Unless you have to be on the cutting edge of what's hot right now in the fashion world, a dress from last year will suit you fine, and you might even find yourself a real bargain. Allowing yourself plenty of time for this project also means that you'll be able to check out dresses all over town, in bridal shops, department stores, and boutiques.

Another reason you should start looking for your dress as soon as the bride has set the wedding date is so that you have time to try different styles and colors and find out what looks best on you. If you put off finding your dress until a month before the wedding, you'll choose whatever's available—and not what flatters your shape and skin tone. You will be on display at the wedding, so you want to look your absolute best.

 Fact

Shopping can really tire some people out. Take care of yourself before and after you go on the hunt for your MOB dress. Get a good night's sleep, take a break when you're feeling weary, and don't shop when you're in a bad mood.

Defining the Perfect Dress

What are you looking for, exactly? Something that blends with the bride's chosen colors. Most moms use the bridesmaids' dresses as a palette. If their gowns are green, you shouldn't choose a pink dress. A different shade of green or even a dress in a complementary shade of blue would be a better choice. You want to avoid white, ivory, black, red, anything too bright (like an electric-blue gown), and anything too overdone.

Although black is becoming more acceptable for MOBs and guests alike to wear to weddings, ask yourself whether you want to be under scrutiny for the color of your dress (no matter how progressive the fashion world is becoming,

MOBs who wear black are always suspected of harboring some ill will toward the union), or you'd rather have guests compliment you for how you look in a particular dress.

Save Your Sanity

Go to lunch. Go to dinner. Make a day (or two) of it. If you're hitting a lot of shops and you fear you won't remember where you saw which dress, take a notebook along and write down a description of each dress alongside the name and address of the store. Knowing that she tried on the perfect dress somewhere—but she can't remember where—is enough to make the MOB decide to wear shorts and flip-flops to the reception.

If you know anyone who has recently played the role of MOB, ask her about her dress-shopping experience. She might be able to steer you in the right direction—or away from a less-than-terrific shop—and save you some time in the process.

Take a friend along for the ride so that you can also get an honest assessment of how the dress looks on you from someone who doesn't stand to make a commission from the sale. You'll want someone to tell you if the dress you love from the front is less than flattering from the rear, and you'll also want a truthful opinion of the style and color, so make sure your shopping companion is an honest woman.

Frugality Is a Virtue (Isn't It?)

Maybe you walk into the first dress shop on your list and you find it—the dress, the one you were imagining, the one that makes you look twenty pounds slimmer and ten years younger. One problem: it costs twice as much as you wanted to spend. Oh, but it's worth it, isn't it? You are the MOB, and you do have to look your best.

❗ Alert

If you're even considering spending far more than you originally planned on a certain dress, take a day or two to make your decision. You may decide that it's worth it, or that the dress made you temporarily lose your mind, but you'll be less likely to suffer buyer's remorse.

This is very true, but you don't have to spend way too much to look great. Know what you're willing to spend before you walk through the doors of a dress shop, and stick with that figure. Spending a little more when you find the perfect dress is all right, but blowing your budget entirely isn't wise, unless it's a dress that you really, truly can wear again and again and again. But before you make yourself that promise (the same promise made by one-time dress wearers all over the world, by the way), ask yourself where you'll wear it.

If there's another wedding coming up in your family, chances are you'll end up buying a new dress for that event (because your kids don't want you wearing the same dress to both weddings). If it's a very formal dress, and you're planning on wearing it to the many formal events you'll be attending in the next year, make sure you won't be seeing the same crowd at those gatherings, or they'll wonder whether you wear that dress to bed, too.

If you'll be attending several weddings and several formal events (and you're 100 percent positive that this dress isn't going to scream "mother of the bride approaching!" and you won't be seeing the same people at each affair), then perhaps it's wise to invest a little more in a dress. Otherwise, resign yourself to the fact that you will most likely wear this dress once, and don't go completely overboard price-wise.

Seamstresses Versus Bridal Shops

If you can't find what you're looking for in a shop, or if you have found exactly what you want but you're not willing to pay the bridal shop's prices, you might look into hiring a seamstress to create your one-of-a-kind MOB dress. Still unsure about handing over the duties to one woman? The dress shop at least has other dresses on the premises in case disaster strikes. Is dealing with one safer than the other? Not really. There are pros and cons to seamstresses and dress shops.

Ask anyone who knows a great seamstress: She's worth every cent she'll charge you for her labor if you just can't buy clothes off the rack or if you can't find anything suitable—as long as the two of you can communicate effectively. This means that you have to be willing to spell out exactly what you want without being overly demanding and unrealistic. She'll tell you if she's not capable of producing the dress you're asking for in the time frame you're giving her, but it may well be that no one (at least no human) can whip up a hand-beaded, full-length gown in a week's time.

 Fact

> Be very careful when you choose a seamstress. If something happens and your dress is not completed as promised, you might find yourself running to the mall or to a dress shop anyway, and you'll have to haggle with the seamstress for a refund.

A good seamstress usually has her hands full—you're probably not her one and only client—and she only has the one set of hands and a given number of hours in any one day to work with. Give your seamstress a call at least six to eight months prior to the wedding, or even sooner if you know she's in high demand.

The advantage to patronizing a dress shop, of course, is that you can try on the dresses and get an idea of how each one looks before you buy one (no such luck with a seamstress). Most bridal shops and high-end dress shops have tailors who will make sure that your dress fits as it should. You'll pay extra for this service, of course. The disadvantage of buying off the rack is that the dresses in these shops can be very expensive, and you're limited to their selection.

"Hello, My Dress Is Pink"

Yes, you're supposed to call the groom's mom and let her in on all of the exciting news of your dress-shopping extravaganza so that she can choose her dress . . . and so that she doesn't choose the same dress. (Horrors!) This is another good reason for you to get started early, because tradition states that the groom's mother has to wait for you to make your selection before she can make hers. She'll start getting pretty irritated if you've put off the dress shopping until three weeks before the wedding. That irritation might just spill over into an ugly MOB-versus-MOG confrontation, which can be avoided altogether if you simply get on the ball and pick out your dress at least two months prior to the ceremony.

The Bride's Dress

Aside from choosing your own dress for the ceremony, there will be the small matter of the bride finding her gown. Depending on your relationship with your daughter, you may be called upon to assist her in the hunt, or she may not want you within a two-mile radius of the dress shop she's visiting. Some moms and daughters have a very hard time shopping together. Add the stress of a wedding to this situation, and a bride may honestly fear that she and her mother won't be speaking to each other at the end of a very long shopping day.

If she does want your help, and you do tend to be a bit excitable or your comments tend to be very blunt, try to cool your heels a bit and remember that the bride is probably more emotional than usual right now. She's embarking on the hunt for the dress she's dreamed of since she was a little girl. Be very careful with your comments.

Shops or Warehouses?

A bride who is looking for a traditional, big, white gown will often begin her search in a bridal shop. Most of these stores require appointments. The dresses are large and unwieldy, and an employee of the store will be dispatched to carry the gowns from the rack to the dressing room, and to assist the bride as she tries on dress after dress after dress. Bottom line: plan ahead, and don't expect to be welcomed with open arms if you're popping in off the street.

Of course, these days, a bride can alternatively head to a bridal warehouse or even shop online for her dress. Is it wise to patronize these businesses? After all, a bride can save herself a bundle, but what are the risks?

🅰️ Alert

Warehouse dresses may be damaged. The bride needs to carefully inspect any dress she's considering for loose threads, tears, missing beads, stains, and the like. She should also get the store's policy on returns *in writing* before she takes her dress out of the store.

If a bride can tolerate the no-frills atmosphere of a warehouse setting, she might just walk away with a bargain. There will be no plush dressing room, no beverages, no store employees catering to her needs. She'll have to hunt through the racks herself to find the perfect dress. However, before your daughter gets too excited about the amount of money she's saving by forgoing the personal service, you should advise her that when she buys a dress from a warehouse, she will be responsible for finding a seamstress for any alterations and/or repairs, an expense that may just defeat the purpose of buying off the rack.

Buying online comes with its own set of worries. Most online bridal shops (and auctions) do not allow returns, and since it's impossible to try on a dress in cyberspace, purchasing a gown this way is very risky. Even if your daughter knows the exact dress she's looking for, she's better off giving her business—and her money—to a local shop. If something goes wrong with the order or the dress, it will be much easier for her to get her point across (i.e., someone had better fix the problem quickly or risk the wrath of the bride) when she's dealing with a real, live person standing in front of her in a dress shop instead of a website.

Make a Game Plan

Shopping for a bride's gown can be an exhausting, head-spinning experience. Unless she finds the dress she's looking for on your first day out, you may find that all of the frocks she's trying on are starting to look very similar. Where once you could differentiate between a quality gown and a cheap one, you're having trouble seeing past the tulle and the beads, and you're leaning toward a dress you suspect you might hate.

How might you avoid shopping overload and confusion before it starts? Sit down with your daughter before you visit your first bridal shop and discuss what she wants versus what might not work. For example, if your daughter is very pale, pure white may not be the right color for her. She might look best in an off-white dress or something with a little color added to it. The hottest style may not be the best pick for her shape; there are far too many brides out there who go for the current trend instead of considering what looks best on them.

Look Away!

So you've put your time in—schlepping from shop to shop, discussing the merits of silk versus chiffon, debating whether white or eggshell is a better color on her, oohing and ahhing over the best gowns—and your daughter has chosen the most unflattering dress she tried on. And she loves it. What are you supposed to do now? Take a week off from shopping so that both of you can mull things over. When you return to the shop, she may notice the obvious flaws in her decision.

 Essential

There is a right way to tell your daughter that a dress doesn't look good on her ("Honey, I think that this other style is very slimming, and this dress you have on isn't.") and a wrong way ("That dress makes your butt look even bigger than it is. Now put on the other one.").

If it's a matter of style—the dress makes her look very heavy, for example, or it makes her look gaunt, or the color just drains the life from her cheeks—these are things you're right to point out to her. They will show in the wedding pictures, and she'll realize too late that this dress didn't suit her at all.

If, on the other hand, this is just a difference of taste (yours versus hers), you need to hold your tongue. You might hate all the beading on the dress she's chosen, or you might have an objection to the length of the train. As long as the gown she's chosen doesn't look horrible on her (there's a very fine line here, and you may have to overcome your personal aversion to certain fabrics or styles), there's no valid reason for her not to wear it to her wedding. You may state your opinion once—nicely—then drop it.

Time to Accessorize!

She'll also be shopping for a headpiece and/or veil, and she really should try these on with her gown. Headpieces are meant to accentuate the gown, not vice versa. If she's chosen a very plain gown, her headpiece shouldn't weigh ten pounds and be covered with gaudy decorations. The only way to be absolutely sure that the headpiece and gown will complement each other is to shop for them simultaneously.

Buyer Be *Very* Wary

You may have heard that some bridal shops run scams on their customers. How can you protect yourself (and your daughter) from falling prey to these nefarious shopkeepers? Your first line of defense is to get a personal recommendation from a friend or acquaintance who has dealt with this particular business recently (you want to know that you're not dealing with new management and new store policies). Take that recommendation with a grain of salt: Though your friend might have had a wonderful relationship with this store, her experience doesn't guarantee that you'll come away without a single complaint.

Has She Grown *That* Much?

The most common bridal shop scam out there involves excessive alterations. Many bridal shops make a lot of money from tailoring dresses—and the more alterations that need to be done on a certain dress, the more money in the cash register.

 Alert

> Bridal shops battle each other for customers, which is one reason tags are sometimes removed from dresses. Shop A certainly doesn't want to make it easy for your daughter to compare the price of the same dress at Shop B. (Removing tags from new garments is illegal, by the way.)

Make sure that when your daughter tries on a dress it has a dress-size tag in it. Some shops remove these tags to prevent brides from gleaning any pertinent information from them (such as the size, the designer, or the style number). How is this a scam? Let's say your daughter wears a size 10 dress. She slips on the floor model of a gown that seems to fit perfectly, but there's no tag to indicate what size she has on, so a shop employee can tell her that the dress she's currently wearing is a size 14, and this particular line of dresses tends to run small. Your daughter orders the dress in a 14, thinking it will fit like a dream, only to find when it arrives—surprise, surprise—that it's hanging off her and she'll need extensive alterations to make it fit the way it should.

Alterations on a wedding gown are not always a scam and are actually often necessary. In addition, many gowns really do run smaller than the average off-the-rack, everyday dress. When the tag is missing from the sample dress, though, you should be suspicious (because you have no way to tell what size it really is, and you're trusting an employee whom you don't know to be truthful).

More Shop Shams

Other things to watch for and avoid when doing business with a dress shop:

- **Don't allow the dress to be shipped to your home.** You want the shop to be ultimately responsible for securing the bride's dress; you and your daughter have enough to worry about.
- **Don't put more than 50 percent down at the time the dress is ordered.** Even for special orders, reputable stores will not require more than half of the full payment.
- **Don't pay deposits in cash.** Again, no reputable store will demand cash payment. Using your credit card is your safest bet.
- **Read the contract.** Make sure everything is spelled out—the price, the size of the dress, the manufacturer

or designer, the order date, the delivery date, any extra charges or discounts, and any special instructions (e.g., long sleeves instead of short).

Rest assured, most bridal shops are on the up-and-up, but it's important to have a little knowledge of the darker side of the business so that you and your daughter don't end up with horrible memories of this experience. Before plunking down money for your daughter's wedding dress, check the Better Business Bureau's website (*www.bbb .org*) to see if there are any complaints against the shop you're considering doing business with and, of course, search the Internet.

MOB Beauty and Pampering

The bride is the not the only one who needs some beauty pampering the day of the wedding. You get to have a little of the glory, too! Try to treat yourself by getting the same beauty treatments your daughter will receive, like a manicure, pedicure, and hair and makeup styling. Another great idea is to treat yourself to a massage—something you deserve after all the planning and stress. You should find out whether or not the bride will want to do these day-before and day-of spa treatments with you or with her bridesmaids. Don't be offended if she wants time alone with her bridesmaids—this is her last spa day with her girls before she becomes a "Mrs." and she may need the time to relax and focus before the big day.

CHAPTER 9

Delicate Situations

*W*eddings bring people together for a joyous occasion, but they also increase the potential for conflict and uncomfortable situations. If your daughter decided to have a big wedding, and there have been issues in the past with family members or friends, you'll need to be prepared to handle these issues calmly and with dignity. You may be forced to reckon with the past—or perhaps a less-than-pleasant set of current circumstances. Former husbands, relatives you thought were long gone, and steprelations will be popping up all over the place. You'll be happy to see some of them, no doubt . . . but what do you do with the others?

Family Dynamics

If you divorced your husband years ago, by now the two of you may have worked out a peaceful (if distant) coexistence. The kids haven't heard the two of you argue with each other in a decade or more, and your lives are completely separate at this point. Even if you aren't exactly the best of friends, this is a somewhat amicable relationship. You are better off apart, and your children are happier for it, too. If this describes you, the wedding plans will most likely proceed without a lot of infighting or backstabbing.

If, on the other hand, the divorce was more recent and there are still unresolved issues between you and the man who used to be your spouse, this wedding could take your relationship from bad to worse. Why? A daughter's wedding is an emotional experience for people who are feeling fairly stable in their lives; it goes without saying that it can be extremely emotional for parents who are at odds with one another.

Mr. Moneybags

Money is a huge flash point in many divorces. If your ex-husband owes you a bundle from the sale of joint property, for example, and he's been dragging his feet on cutting you a check, you may have very mixed emotions when he sweeps into town offering to pay for your daughter's entire wedding. He's her hero right now, regardless of their prior relationship. Sure, you're happy that she's going to get the wedding she's always dreamed of, but you're scraping by every month. You can't afford to contribute much at this point, which makes you feel awful, but if your ex would just hand over the money you're owed, you could come off looking like a super parent, too.

 Alert

The last thing you want to do is to get your child tangled up in the financial mess that often follows a divorce. You especially wouldn't want to make the bride feel as though you begrudge her the money her father is so generously offering.

What do you do when your ex isn't playing fair with the wedding finances? Sit back and watch as money that is rightfully yours is spent on flowers and bonbons, while you rack up more and more life-related debt? Your best bet is to shut down any chance of this happening in the first place. When your daughter first becomes engaged, let your ex know that you won't allow him to throw money at her until he's given you what's yours. This is not a matter of pettiness, as you well know—it's a matter of fairness and a matter of necessity, as well. Chances are, one way or the other, your daughter is going to have a splendid wedding. It would be nice, though, if you and her dad could both be benefactors of the big day.

The New Mrs.

Your ex-husband has a new wife in his life, and she seems to have definite ideas for your daughter's wedding. Unless you and your ex's wife are friendly with each other (which is not an uncommon situation, though you should still consider yourself lucky if the two of you can be civil to each other), you might find yourself preparing to go head-to-head with her over the menu, the reception site, and the guest list. This is not how you envisioned your role as MOB—you thought you would be the only MOB.

First, you have to take stock of what's really going on between you and your ex's new wife. If the two of you have a long-standing feud, trying to co-plan a wedding is going to be difficult at best. Because weddings are such an emotional time, there's a chance that you'll be more irritated than usual with each other as you try to compromise without really giving in to her (or her to you) on anything. On the other hand, this could be a perfect time for you two to finally realize what's important (your daughter is important enough to both of you that you want to make sure the wedding is beautiful) and what isn't (namely, the past).

Another thing to consider is how much each of you is throwing into the wedding pot. While it may not seem fair to you if your ex-husband is paying for most of this wedding, his wife does have a right to pipe up now and then regarding the details. If the bride has a real problem with her stepmother's opinions, that's a whole separate issue, and the way to handle it is unique to each family. Your daughter might feel comfortable putting her foot down on certain issues, she may appeal to her father, or she just might ask you to intervene on her behalf.

Unless you and the stepmother are on good terms, this is a risky proposition. Nothing good will come of your middleman approach; in fact, it will probably make things much worse all the way around, for many reasons:

- Your ex's wife will feel that you and your daughter are teaming up against her.
- Your ex will be forced to actively choose a side. Family turmoil will follow.
- These are the types of fights that go on forever, precisely because the atmosphere surrounding a wedding is so emotional.

Implore your daughter to act like an adult and be assertive with her stepmother, or appeal to her dad.

The Bride's Stepdad

Your husband is a man among men. He happens to be the bride's stepfather, and she also happens to be very close to her "real" dad. You fear that someone's feelings are going to be hurt along the way, because, after all, only one of these men can escort her down the aisle, right? How can you persuade her to choose your husband, who is, after all, the dad who's physically been around all of these years? Many brides are having both their father and stepfather walk them down the aisle if the bride is close to both. Leave this decision in your daughter's hands and she will typically know how to relay the news to both father and stepfather.

This is completely the bride's choice, and no matter what's happened between you and her dad (or her and her dad) over the years, she shouldn't be pressured or guilted into choosing one man over the other. Even if you think she's making a wrong choice and basing it on sentimentality, zip the lip. It's her wedding, and this is what she wants. This is one thing that is absolutely not up to you to criticize or attempt to influence.

 Fact

If the bride's father is deceased, she may choose to have one of her brothers escort her down the aisle, even if you remarried years ago. A stepfather should walk her down the aisle only if it's her choice, and only if they're close.

Unless your former and current husbands have huge issues to work out (one has stolen money from the other, or one has stolen a wife from the other), they may be content to leave each other alone and get on with life. If your husband and your ex have very little to do with each other and barely acknowledge each other's existence, you can't expect them to act chummy at the reception; just be thankful they're not roping off the dance floor for a fight to the finish.

An Ex-Family Reunion

Depending on the circumstances, you may or may not have a good relationship with your ex-husband. Whether you can't stand the man (or the new wife) or you have an amicable relationship with your ex, take charge and be the better lady for the day!

The Dreaded "Ex" Factor

If you are sitting there with a pit in your stomach thinking about your ex-husband and his family at the wedding, then this section is for you. If his family has "Tommy the Terrible" as your daughter's uncle and your ex's sister is the "Wicked Witch of the West," fear not—you are the mother of the bride! Yep, that's right—you are the First Lady for the day and you should keep it that way with *your* behavior.

If this were your wedding, you could completely discard these folks and surround yourself with people who would only heap praise and compliments on you for the entire day. Of course, this isn't your day, no matter how much money and energy you've put into it. Your former relations are your daughter's blood relatives, and as long as she's not actively doing battle with them, you have to respect that bond. You can't exclude your former mother-in-law, because as far as your daughter is concerned, she's Grandma. What's happened between the two of you must be put aside for one day.

You'll be incredibly busy on the day of the wedding, looking out for your daughter and making sure that everything's going according to plan, and you won't have time to worry about what your former brother-in-law might be saying about you at any given moment—so don't!

If this is a particularly new situation for you, your daughter will be keenly aware and will want to make sure everyone is comfortable that day. It is your job, as her mom, to suck it up for the wedding weekend. Yes, this is the harsh reality you will have to face. Don't ruin your daughter's chances of having a wonderful and worry-free wedding due to your hurt feelings—you will never forgive yourself later. Your daughter already knows the hurt and the heartache because she is probably hurt by the situation as well. Assure your daughter that you will be on your best behavior and that the day is all about her and her fiancé and not about your divorce. Be sure to relay this to your ex (if possible), so he will be on his best behavior as well.

Take Control

If someone from the "other" side of the family decides to cause a ruckus, remain in control (do not blow a fuse!). Unfortunately, some folks go out of their way to start trouble by initiating face-to-face confrontations. A wedding is one of the least appropriate places to revisit old arguments. Your best bet is to simply ignore anyone who tries to pull you into a fight. If the behavior is really out of bounds (shouting, cursing, etc.), you have every right to ask the troublemaker to leave. Your daughter and her groom (and his entire family) shouldn't have to bear witness to such ugliness on their big day. You can also tactfully suggest seating arrangements to your daughter. Your daughter probably knows you better than anyone else and will in turn do her best to protect you (and her wedding) from troublesome encounters.

The Dreaded New Wife

There you are, sitting at the dining room table contemplating the table assignments. You then realize that the "new" wife—yep, the one who is now married to your ex-husband—will be at the wedding. Again, be the better lady here and include her as much as your daughter wants to include her. If your daughter wants a corsage for her, get her one. If the bride-to-be wants the new wife to sit in the front row next to her dad, let her. The one place you can really draw the line is with table assignments. You don't have to sit at the table with your ex and his new wife. Make sure he has his family surrounding him at his table and you have your family (or friends) surrounding you at your table. It's that simple. You can't stop her from coming to the wedding. You will have to focus on the fact that you are the mom and nothing should detract from your daughter's big day.

Amicable Ex-Husband

If you are one of the lucky few, you have a good relationship with your ex-husband. This is a true blessing for the day of the wedding, as it will really help keep the bride and the groom worry-free. Try to include her father in as many ways as possible, as your daughter still sees you as her mom and dad (divorced or not).

Step Right Up, Calling All Stepmothers!

When your stepdaughter gets engaged, what's your official title? Are you the SMOB (stepmother of the bride)? Are you responsible for anything, as far as this wedding is concerned, or does most of the work fall squarely on the shoulders of your husband's former wife? As weddings veer further and further off the traditional track, you'll find that every situation involving a stepmother and a bride-to-be is unique.

Your involvement in the wedding will depend on your stepdaughter's relationship with her dad, her relationship with her mother, and her relationship with you. Proceed with the utmost caution, and no one will be able to criticize your moves.

 Alert

> Remember that the bride is going through this process for the first time. She might forget about you altogether, not because she wants to insult you, but because it hasn't occurred to her to include you. Don't take it personally; it is typical for a bride to want to do the planning either all by herself or with her mom.

Stepmom Straits

Your stepdaughter has come home wearing an engagement ring. Your husband is planning on paying for most of the wedding. Where do you fit in now? Some concerns a stepmother of the bride may have include:

- Your duties. Are you the hostess, or simply the wife of the host?
- The finances. Is the bride's mom the official sponsor of the reception, although the checks have been written out of your joint account?
- The invitations. Can you invite your family, or is that tacky?

When the split was amicable and both of the bride's parents are involved in the wedding, most brides will send out an invitation that includes the names of both sets of parents, indicating co-hosting. As far as inviting your family, you'll want to consider whether they have anything to do with your stepdaughter. If your brother barely knows the bride, for example, she may wonder why he's being included in the celebration of her marriage.

Are You In or Out?

Will you be called on to help with the planning? You might be, especially if you have some interesting connections in town (say, your best friend is a florist, or you happen to know a world-class violinist who just might be talked into soloing at the ceremony), but you might not be. If you're very, very close to your stepdaughter, she'll probably be sensitive enough to realize that excluding you from the planning could be very hurtful to you. If the two of you get along pretty well but aren't exactly soulmates, she may simply lean on her mom.

The Wedding Day

Depending on what your stepdaughter chooses, you will have to wait until the rehearsal or the day of the wedding to figure out where you will be seated during the ceremony. At the reception, you may not be required to stand in the receiving line. Regardless, get inside, greet the guests as they enter the area set up with cocktails and appetizers, and be a gracious co-hostess. Touch base with the bride's mom now and then to see if you can lend a hand somewhere, but don't steal her limelight. That advice goes double for your dress: Choose something that complements the bride's mother's gown but that doesn't completely upstage her. Find a way to ask her about (and be interested in) what she is wearing.

Keeping the Peace

As if working out the roles for mothers, stepmothers, fathers, and stepfathers wasn't difficult enough, it has suddenly occurred to you that all of you will be under one roof at the ceremony and reception (and possibly at several parties before the wedding). To top it off, the groom's parents are also divorced, and their situation is not what anyone would call friendly.

 Essential

Your daughter has already lived through your divorce once. Don't reopen old wounds by exchanging nastiness with your ex now. Regardless of your own experience, do your best to make sure that your daughter enters into marriage thinking it's a *good* thing.

Is it in everyone's best interest to simply keep the prewedding parties separate and to graciously exclude one parent from each family from the reception? That would make life so much easier, but it's really not appropriate to decide that one parent has to miss his or her child's wedding. All of the parents concerned are adults and should be held to adult standards of conduct.

Pre-Wedding Parties

If there's a horrific split in the family (between you and the bride's father, or between the groom's parents), it's best to keep the guest list for any pre-wedding parties as small and as simple as possible. If you're hosting a small engagement party, for example, you don't need to invite your ex and his new wife and their entire extended families. The bride's father always has the option of hosting a separate engagement celebration.

Showers should also be handled tactfully. If your divorce set off a series of rumblings in your ex's family (and the result is that you are not welcome in their homes, and they are not welcome in yours), there's no sense in trying to push everyone together for an afternoon of forced niceties (or worse, an afternoon of sparring). Since showers are not required to have a bridesmaid as hostess in this day and age, your ex's family is more than welcome to host their own shower for the bride.

At the Ceremony

Keeping everyone apart for the duration of the engagement is one thing: There can be multiple, separate parties for the bride and groom at which former family members need never cross paths. Not so with the wedding ceremony. The bride usually only gets one ceremony, and it's up to her (and you) to figure out a way to keep the peace over the course of the day.

In the case of a nasty divorce, the FOB may still escort his daughter down the aisle, but he will most likely be seated in the third row, while the MOB and her hubby (if she has remarried) are seated in the first row. If your daughter chose to live with her dad after the divorce, she may flip-flop these seating arrangements so that he has the front-row view of the ceremony (along with her stepmother, if there's a new wife on the scene). Accept this if it happens; it's an approved law of etiquette, not a move designed to hurt or humiliate you. However, more brides have leaned toward having all sets of parents in the first row. Just be sure to ask the bride what she wants before you put in your two cents!

Imagine yourself as the bride. Imagine your own parents embroiled in a nasty, ongoing feud that has yet to show any signs of weakening. Now imagine you're standing at that altar, ready to take your own vows, and all you can think about is whether your mom or dad is going to say something horrible to the other one at any moment. This is the entire reason for the first row/third row separation of combative parents.

At the Reception

With all the milling around that goes on during receptions, an ex is bound to cross paths with his or her former better half. The new wife and the former wife will eventually run into each other in the ladies' room or on the dance floor. The former husband and the current husband will bump elbows at the bar. Are there rules for how these people should interact?

In fact, there are. The rules are called common sense. No matter how much your ex-husband gets under your skin, your daughter's wedding is neither the time nor the place to correct his flaws. If his new wife is shimmying shamelessly all over the dance floor, just remember that her actions don't reflect upon you, and it's really not up to you to stop her squirming.

 Alert

Get creative with the seating arrangements without getting nasty. Seat the bride's father as close to the head table as possible, so that he's still in a place of honor but with at least one group between your table and his. Seating him near the broom closet is just not nice.

While the dance floor, the bar, and the powder room are areas beyond your control, you can make sure that dinner is a pleasant experience for everyone by giving fractured families lots of room to relax. If you've had a particularly bitter split with the bride's father, for example, you may literally feel sick when you look at him. Make sure you won't have to—and especially not while you're eating. Seat your ex and his family several tables away from you.

Special Roles

Godparents and grandparents are often recognized as VIPs during a wedding ceremony. Grandparents should be seated toward the front, and the groom's grandparents are shown to their seats before the bride's grandma and grandpa. The bride and groom often order boutonnieres for the grandfathers and corsages for the grandmothers. Grandparents are seated near the head table at the reception, often with the parents of the bride or groom.

If your daughter has kept a close relationship with her godparents, she may want to ask them to be a part of the ceremony. She may also order a corsage for her godmother or a boutonniere for her godfather. If she hasn't seen these people since she was baptized, however, and they haven't made any special effort to keep her on the straight and narrow by teaching her about her religion, they don't require any special recognition (or even an invitation, for that matter).

Other Important Guests

Your daughter may be especially close to your sister or her father's sister (or any number of other people in her life). Anyone who is a special part of your daughter's life is fair game to be part of the ceremony. Think about suggesting to your daughter that she include these special people in the ceremony somehow, but don't feel shocked if she decides that she just wants to keep it simple.

Second Weddings

You thought your daughter's first time down the aisle would also be her last, but you were wrong. As if educating yourself on how to run the first wedding wasn't enough, now you're faced with a second wedding, and you have no idea how to handle the particulars. Should the bride have another huge wedding if she wants one? Is it really inappropriate for her to walk down the aisle, to have her dad give her away, for her to wear white?

The Size and Shape of Things

Traditional etiquette states that a second wedding ceremony should be an intimate affair, whether the bride or groom has been widowed or divorced. Where death has ended a union, a small second ceremony shows respect for the dearly departed; when the bride or groom has been divorced, etiquette mavens encourage a quiet second wedding to discourage less-than-kind onlookers from pointing out that one of the interested parties has already broken the very vows that he or she is reciting again.

If your daughter wants another big wedding this time around, chances are her decision will be based on more practical matters (such as money and how many guests she wants to invite) than on the ins and outs of social graces. This is another example of opting for nontraditional practices.

 Question

Can a bride wear white to her second wedding?
Traditional etiquette would say no; white is a symbol of purity and is supposed to signify a virgin bride. However, second-time brides are not held to this rigid rule nowadays. Trains are frowned upon at the second wedding (unless a family heirloom or special gift of a veil is given), though; suits and tea-length and floor-length gowns are popular choices.

If the bride has chosen to have a quiet ceremony, she may have only one or two attendants. The bride herself may choose to wear a simple gown or a bridal suit instead of a wedding gown. What will you wear, then? Follow the bride's lead. If she's chosen something knee-length and fairly understated, your dress should be even more understated. (In other words, don't try to sneak into the ceremony wearing a floor-length, beaded gown while the bride is dressed in a tea-length, off-the-rack dress. Someone is going to notice that you're more done-up than your daughter is.)

Who's Got the Check?

The bride and groom usually pay for a second wedding and list themselves as hosts on the invitations. If you and your husband would like to contribute to the wedding or reception, no one will stop you; however, if your daughter had a big wedding the first time around and you have no intention of handing over one cent for this event, hardly anyone will fault you for that decision (except, perhaps, your daughter).

Don't make the money issue a personal matter between you and the bride. If you thought she made a huge mistake in either marrying or divorcing her first husband, the worst thing you could do right now is to tell her, "I will not pay for your second wedding, because you should have stayed married to Bill in the first place!" She's in a specific position in life; she can't go back in time and change the events that brought her to this point. You don't have to pay for a second wedding, but don't bring her judgment into question now.

The Kids

If your daughter has children, should they be at the second wedding? You want to shield your grandkids from any discomfort, and if the little ones (or not-so-little ones) aren't exactly thrilled about the prospect of acquiring a stepfather, shouldn't they just stay home instead?

 Fact

> Many brides and grooms include their children in a second wedding ceremony. In addition to making the kids feel important for an afternoon, encouraging the feeling that they're all in this together can go a long way toward easing the transition to being an actual family.

Even if your daughter's children aren't happy about their mom's wedding, they should be there. Her marriage vows will take them into a new reality, whether they like it or not, and the worst way to start off that new life is to boycott this event. Do everything in your power to convince older kids that they should be at the ceremony and reception, because if they're allowed to skip it, everyone is instantly put into an awkward position. Your daughter's husband will feel insulted and/or angry, the kids will be at odds with their new stepfather, and your daughter will be in the middle. There will be lots of time to work out the big issues after the wedding. For now, everyone needs to show support for one another—even if it hurts a little.

Same-Sex Weddings

If you have never been to a same-sex wedding and your daughter is happily engaged to a woman, know that you don't have to change much of your planning process. However, there are a few guidelines that should be followed and some new traditions that can make the planning process easier and more fun.

Two MOBs

You may ask, "Who gets to be MOB Number One?" In your daughter's mind, you are MOB Number One, and her fiancé feels the same way about her mother. You get to have the same privileges of being the mother of the bride as anyone else whose daughter gets engaged. The best part of this situation is that you get to have double the advice giving *and* gain a daughter in the process.

Who Pays for What?

Now that you have two brides, traditional etiquette could change drastically when it comes to figuring out who should pay for what. The most popular view is that with two brides going down the aisle, both sets of parents should be willing to help split the costs evenly (if it is the first wedding for both of them).

However, not everyone has the same budget guidelines (just like every other modern wedding). You, your daughter, her fiancé, and her fiancé's mother will need to meet and discuss a plan. Get together with no real expectations and be ready to listen and see where everyone's budget is. You may have a large amount to spend or none at all. Her fiancé's mother may be in the same boat as you. Communication is the key, just as it is for any other wedding.

 **Essential**

Ensure Your Daughter's Happiness

If you have decided that you do not agree with the lifestyle your daughter has chosen, be very careful. In no way does this excuse you from being at your daughter's wedding. No matter what your views are about your daughter's choice of a partner in life, you need to be at your daughter's wedding and keep any negative comments to yourself. Remember, you are not the one getting married—your daughter's happiness is most important. Both brides have been dreaming about finding the love of their lives, and both want to have a dream wedding.

It has been your job as a mother to protect your daughter her entire life. You may not agree with everything your daughter does, but being a mother does not mean agreeing all the time. Make sure you do not invite guests who you know would disapprove of the marriage. Your daughter's wedding day is not the time to become political, to start arguments, or to brood. Keep your daughter's wedding the way she wants it—a happy and memorable day—regardless of your opinion.

Questions to Ask

There are a couple of specific questions you will need to ask when planning your daughter's same-sex wedding:

- **Is it legal?** First things first! You and your daughter will need to figure out whether or not your daughter's gay marriage will be legal. Laws are changing constantly and you want to stay informed. Stay on top of this with social media. You can stay up to date on your smartphone with one of the best apps on the market for gay weddings, the 14 Stories Gay Wedding Confidential app. This app provides an up-to-date list of states where gay marriage is legal. You may want to consider advising your daughter about the locations where gay marriage is legal. She may want to get legally married in one state (if your state does not recognize same-sex marriage) and then have a reception in your hometown (or host the reception in the same state as the ceremony).

- **Have you worked with same-sex couples before?** Yes, you have to ask all of your vendors this question. The last thing you want is a vendor that is not familiar with gay weddings. You especially need to ask any photographers and videographers you are considering this question, since they will be around your daughter and future daughter-in-law all day long! If any vendor is uncomfortable with the question, move on to the next vendor, as you really need to find gay-friendly vendors.

New Gay Wedding Traditions

Like all weddings, gay weddings have started to take on their own traditions. Here are a few of the most popular.

- **Champagne!** More than just a drink for toasting, many same-sex weddings start with a little pre-ceremony champagne for the guests. Keep in mind that it is only in very recent history that gay weddings have become legal and that this is a big deal. Starting off the day by popping the cork is the best way to set the mood.
- **The processional.** Since there are two brides at this wedding, both will want to come down the aisle. There are two camps here: You can have both come down the aisle together or create two separate aisles for them to meet in the middle. Depending on what the brides want, they may want their fathers to go down the aisle with them. Finding a unique way to make this happen is all part of making this grand entrance!
- **Toast the guests.** Your daughter is now married and so happy to have her closest friends and family present for her big day. Here comes one of the best traditions in gay weddings: The newlyweds will make a toast to the guests, thanking them for their support. This can occur before or after toasts from family and attendants.

There are other traditions that your daughter and future daughter-in-law may want to incorporate into their big day. Find out their hearts' desires and help make it happen!

CHAPTER 10

The Guest List

epending on the size of the wedding, you may have an easy time whipping up the guest list, or you may find yourself making precise, surgical cuts here and there—and encouraging the groom's family to do the same. If this is a second wedding, you may not know whether it's appropriate to invite the same guests you invited to your daughter's first marriage. And then there's the issue of purchasing and assembling the invitations, which is not an easy task!

One for You, and One for Me . . .

Even if the groom's family isn't taking on a large part of the wedding expenses, they are entitled to invite their friends and relatives to the reception—and they should be allowed to invite roughly as many guests as your family is inviting. Remember, when all is said and done, this is a celebration of your daughter's and their son's marriage, and the groom's parents will want to have their loved ones in attendance, too.

Years ago, the guest list was split evenly between the two families, which made it easy to conjure up the magical number of attendees for each side. However, with more and more couples paying for their own weddings these days, and because more brides and grooms are waiting until they're older to walk down the aisle (and hence have their own group of friends and business associates they might like to include at the reception), the guest list is sometimes split three ways now: One-third of the head count goes to the bride and groom; one-third goes to the bride's family; and the remaining third goes to the groom's family. Everyone's happy, and no one can be accused of commandeering the entire guest list.

Who's In, Who's Out

Before you can even think of drawing up a list of potential reception revelers, you need to think about who should be invited—and who shouldn't. Each family is different, of course, but there are some general guidelines you might want to follow and some advice that may help you out of some pretty hot water down the line. The first thing you need to know is this: If you're hosting a large reception, someone is going to be offended at not being invited or be unhappy about being invited. Unfortunately, this is the nature of the wedding season. You can't please everyone, not even when you try your hardest to do so.

The Family

Obviously, if the reception is a small affair, you'll have to pick and choose between extended family members very carefully. Only those people who have (recently) been very close to you or your daughter would expect to be invited to such an intimate gathering. (In other words, don't feel bad about not being able to invite your best friend from high school, whom you haven't spoken to in several years.)

Many MOBs invite the entire family—aunts, uncles, fourth and fifth cousins, and folks who are only rumored to be blood relatives. Before you go this route, examine your motives. Perhaps your family is huge but extremely close, and by not inviting everyone you'd be breaking the family code of togetherness. Your heart is in the right place if this is your major concern. If, on the other hand, you want a packed house for the sake of appearances, you won't be fooling anyone, especially if this is your regular modus operandi. All the guests there will know why they were invited—if they bother to show at all.

Inviting people you hardly know to your daughter's wedding can be construed as a request for gifts. Many families operate this way; there's a tacit rule of reciprocity there (you bought cousin Jane's daughter a lovely set of candlesticks for her wedding; now it's Jane's turn to pony up), and that's fine. When you start inviting distant relations and long-lost friends who aren't in on this exchange system, though, it's more likely that they'll ask themselves how they made it onto the guest list in the first place.

 **Question**

Should children be invited to a formal wedding?
It's absolutely fine to include close relatives like nephews and nieces. You might also want to consider a cut-off age for kids—but *stick to it*. Don't include your eight-year-old relative and then tell the groom's mom that her ten-year-old nephew is too young.

The Associates

Who hasn't been invited to a business associate's wedding or the wedding of a colleague's child at one time or another? Business relationships can be peculiar. You may work with some people you feel extremely close to, but in the same office there may be folks you barely talk to. Still, you have to work with all of these people every day. You certainly don't want to offend anyone, but you also don't want to come across looking as though you're inviting everyone under the sun so that they'll send your daughter a gift.

The level of difficulty of this situation really depends on how large your workplace is. If your office has 150 people in it, you obviously can't invite everyone, so you're free to include only those you're closest to. If you work in an office of ten employees, though, inviting only six of those people will greatly offend the others—quite possibly for years to come.

Aside from leaving certain coworkers out in the cold, the very issue of a wedding can cause problems in the workplace, such as when the invitees talk in hushed tones about what they're going to wear to the reception, then clam up the second a noninvitee enters the area. Your safest bet in this case is either to invite everyone or to invite no one.

Everybody Else

Should you really invite the entire neighborhood, your hairdresser, the guy who's been plowing your driveway every winter for the past twenty years, your doctor, the mailman, and your accountant? Only if any of them happen to be close friends of yours or of the family. None of these people (or others like them), who are in your life without really being in on it, will expect an invitation—or at least they shouldn't—even if your small talk with them has consisted of nothing but wedding details lately. Most of them would probably find an invitation to your daughter's wedding odd, to say the least.

Guests?

There's been a debate raging for eons as to whether brides should allow their guests to bring guests no matter what the circumstances, or whether each bride should make that decision based on the size and location of her own wedding.

A guest's spouse or fiancé should always be included. Of course, now that many couples live together for years before they become officially engaged or married (if they ever take those steps), the question of inviting a guest's significant other has become more complicated. Consider couples who live together to be as good as engaged, and include both of them on the guest list.

The Second Wedding

You're planning another wedding for your daughter, and, tradition be darned, she wants another big affair. Her reasoning is that while this may be her second trip to the altar, it's her fiancé's first, and he wants a big wedding. She doesn't want her side of the church to be empty, and she wants to see lots of friendly, familiar faces at the reception, so she wants you to break out that address book and invite the usual suspects—again. Is this proper etiquette? Is it any of your business?

The Rule

Etiquette states that a second wedding should be a smaller event than the first one. While many people (perhaps some of your potential guests, even) may agree with this notion, this tradition came about in the age when second marriages were nothing less than scandalous. Nowadays, just about everybody has a human face to put with the word *remarriage*, which has lessened the shock factor of the term considerably.

Still, this is a case-by-case scenario. Some folks tend to have a very rigid view of marriage and remarriage, and if this isn't the bride's first time down the aisle, she's likely to be judged by certain groups as being either morally corrupt or crazy. Generally speaking, if your entire family can best be described as extremely pious, forget about inviting them to the second wedding. Your daughter will spend the day under their moral microscopes, if they decide to come at all.

To Invite or Not to Invite?

So you know the official line of etiquette on the guest list for second weddings. You neither agree nor disagree, and you don't know what you should do. Where do you go from here? You are the best judge of your guests' reactions to being invited to a big second wedding. Will they gossip over the decision to have another big wedding? Will they come? Will they be angry about being expected to give another gift?

 Fact

If you're uncomfortable inviting the entire family to another large wedding, don't do it. If she's bound and determined to invite them anyway, the bride can pay for the wedding herself and put her own name and the groom's on the invitations as sponsors.

If you really have no problem with the situation but you're a little leery about the guests' reactions, remember this advice: You'll never make everyone happy with the wedding guest list, not even for a first wedding. Sometimes, the only thing you can do is to put yourself on the line. Those who are going to be judgmental will be (and they would be even if they weren't invited to the wedding), and those who want to wish the couple well will. You can't intervene and force everyone to accept the invitation and/or the marriage, so send the invitations and let the rest take care of itself.

Former Family Members

Should the bride's ex-in-laws be invited to a second wedding? Probably not. If your daughter's very best friend in the world happens to be her ex-husband's sister, you can make an exception to this rule, but otherwise, keep the exes out of it. It's not common for a bride to remain close to her former in-laws, for one thing, and how will the new groom's family react to being forced to mingle with the former groom's kin?

Not every second marriage is the result of divorce, however. If your daughter is a widow and is planning to remarry, she may have some questions as to what is proper and what isn't. The rule for remarriage after death is the same: a smaller affair this time around, out of respect for her deceased husband.

Should the bride invite her late husband's in-laws? If she's remained close to them, she should. Ideally, they should hear about the wedding from her before they receive an invitation in the mail. If she hasn't spoken to these folks in ages, she really doesn't need to include them in the guest list; it wouldn't make sense to do so.

The B List

Because many reception facilities and caterers will demand a minimum number of guests (or charge you for uneaten meals), and because many brides love big

weddings with lots and lots of onlookers, guest lists sometimes grow like mushrooms to the point where the bride
(or the MOB) is able to make an A list and a B list. The A list
contains the names of the people the bride really wants at
her reception, and the B list is filled with the names of
guests who will do if her favorite folks can't make it. Is this
a safe plan, or a scheme fraught with peril?

 **Essential**

> Thinking of shifting the invites earlier? You won't be
> fooling anyone. Most people have also been invited to
> other weddings at some point and will wonder why your
> daughter's invitations are the only ones to demand such
> an early response.

It's a rude plan, really. Wedding invitations are supposed to
be mailed a minimum of six weeks before the wedding, with
a requested response time of two weeks prior to the event.
These time frames can be shifted only slightly (the invites can
go out as early as eight weeks prior, and the responses can
be requested three weeks before the wedding). Anyone who
has any inkling of wedding invitation etiquette and receives
an invitation a month before the event is going to know that
they weren't on the original guest list.

In the end, some of your B-list invitees are bound to figure out the game, no matter how skilled you are in trying to
pull it off. Before you do a tango with two guest lists, prepare
yourself for the possible consequences. Let's say, for example, that your irritating cousin Darla calls to ask why she has

only just received her invitation to your daughter's wedding when she knows darn well that your favorite cousin, Marla, received hers several weeks ago. You've been caught. She already knows what is going on, and she's forcing you to either be brutally honest or to fabricate some sort of lie.

Be very careful if you're dealing with an A list and a B list. Your intention (hopefully) is not to insult your relatives; however, because weddings tend to illuminate everyone's true colors (including deep-seated issues of insecurity and the ability to hold grudges), you may suffer the consequences of hurt feelings for years to come. If you can't handle the fallout, it may be best to bite the bullet and invite everyone or to cut the guest list along definitive lines (e.g., first cousins are in, second cousins are out).

Selecting the Invitations

Drawing up the guest list is only the beginning of what often proves to be a labor-intensive process. Unless your daughter knows exactly what she wants in the way of invites, the two of you will be faced with oodles of choices, from the paper to the ink to the printing process and style.

Assembling the invitations and addressing them may require you to recruit helpers, and then you'll deal with acceptances, regrets, and guests who simply fail to respond.

Where to Get Invitations

Many wedding planners start their search for the invitations at a printer or a shop (stationery or department store) that offers printing services. These days, the Internet also offers a wide array of choices for those who are comfortable shopping in cyberspace. Unless you are a veritable expert in printing methods and paper, though, you may be better off hitting a shop (at least initially) where you can actually see what the invitations will look and feel like once they're finished.

 Fact

It may be easier to deal with a stationery store in town should you have any problems with the invitations down the line. No matter how good the customer service department of an Internet site may be, a nervous bride may need the reassurance of a human being she can actually *see*.

Invitation catalogs are filled with sample invites that can be customized for your daughter's wedding. Often, she'll have to pick a color, a script style, and a printing method, but the rest of the invitation (the design, the phrasing) is duplicated in the final product. It's a fairly easy process for any bride to get through. If she's looking for something more unique, she may want to visit a print shop and talk to a designer on the premises. She can throw out her ideas and work with the store to create an invitation that suits her specific ideas. Be aware that this will cost more than ordering the invitations out of a catalog.

Technical Matters
There are several printing methods to choose from, and this choice will affect the final cost of the invitations.

Engraving is the most expensive option, so if your daughter has her heart set on the fanciest invitations in town, you may be paying a significant amount for them. Thermography is another option. It produces a raised-letter print that is almost identical to engraving but at a much lower price.

 Essential

Wording the invitation can be a tricky task: If there is more than one host, or the hosts have divorced each other and remarried, how will the invitation reflect this? And how is a traditional invitation worded, anyway? Don't worry—see Appendix B for guidelines and samples.

Many brides love the look of calligraphy; however, hiring a calligrapher to produce hundreds of invitations might not be the most finance-friendly idea. Printers now have access to computer software that can simulate hand-scripted calligraphy at a fraction of the price of hiring a human to do the same job.

Little Extras

Some wedding invitations arrive packed with little inserts. Even if you love or hate the idea of inserts, sometimes they're the best way to let your guests in on certain information. Consider your options:

- **Ceremony cards.** If the wedding is being held in a public place (a museum, for example), you want your guests to be able to scoot past those who are waiting in line to pay admission.

- **Pew cards (or "within-the-ribbon" cards).** Slip these cards into the appropriate invitations if you're planning on reserving the front section of the church for special guests (usually family and the closest friends). The guests will then give them to the ushers, who will seat them in the reserved area.
- **Rain cards.** These cards alert guests to an alternate location if the wedding site could be affected by inclement weather.
- **Response cards and envelopes.** The card includes the date of the requested RSVP; the envelope will have a preprinted return address.
- **Reception cards.** Although you'll be offered the option of printing the reception information on the wedding invitation itself, it's classier to have a separate insert.
- **Envelopes.** Do they need to be foil-lined? No. Ask yourself where the envelopes end up (think trashcan), and go with the less expensive options.
- **Thank-you notes.** Most often, the bride and groom will order cards that complement the wedding invitations. Their married names are usually printed on these cards (whether it's Mr. and Mrs. James Smith or Allison Brown and James Smith).

Putting It All Together

You should order the invitations and all the accompanying inserts a minimum of four months before the wedding, not only so that they will have plenty of time to arrive, but because you'll also need time to put them together into little packages for your guests' enjoyment. When you pick up your order, you'll have everything you ordered, plus tissue paper and envelopes. What goes where and why?

If the invitation is folded, the inserts go inside of the first fold; if the invites are one flat sheet, the inserts go on top. Either way, they go in this order: tissue paper (on top of the printing on the invitation, so that it doesn't smudge), reception card, map, response envelope, response card under the flap of its envelope. All of this goes inside the inner envelope (the envelope with adhesive) with the printed side of the invitation facing the flap.

 Alert

Don't forget the stamps for the reply cards! Have one weighed at the post office to make sure it's standard size, shape, and weight, or you may need extra postage.

Those inner envelopes need to be addressed, too, which is where many brides and MOBs run into difficulty if they're trying to adhere to etiquette standards. So many issues crop up here: Should proper titles be used? Does an entire family living in one house receive a single invitation for the entire family?

Addressing the Envelopes

First of all, if you know the guest in question well, you're free to be as informal as you wish on the inner envelope.

If your brother is an MD, there's no need to address him as Doctor Nolan here—you can simply use his first name. On the other hand, if Dr. Nolan is not a close personal friend, you'd keep his title as is. Be aware that professional titles undergo a metamorphosis when they're moved from the outer envelope to the inner one. See the following table for some examples:

INVITATION ENVELOPE ETIQUETTE

	Outer Envelope	Inner Envelope
Lawyer		
	Mitchell Nolan, Esq.	Mr. Nolan
Physician		
	Ann Nolan, MD	Doctor Nolan (or Doctor Ann Nolan)
Married Physicians		
	Doctors Mitchell and Ann Nolan	The Doctors Nolan
Married Male Physician		
	Doctor and Mrs. Mitchell Nolan	Doctor Nolan and Mrs. Nolan
Married Female Physician		
	Doctor Ann Nolan and Mr. Mitchell Nolan	Doctor Nolan and Mr. Nolan
PhD		
	Dr. Mitchell Nolan	Dr. Nolan
Minister		
	The Reverend Mitchell Nolan	The Reverend Nolan
Catholic Priest		
	Father Mitchell Nolan	Father Nolan

	Outer Envelope	Inner Envelope
Rabbi		
	Rabbi Mitchell Nolan	Rabbi Nolan
Judge		
	The Honorable Ann Nolan	Judge Nolan

Most of these titles allow a spouse to be tacked on fairly easily, such as in the case of The Honorable and Mrs. Mitchell Nolan, or The Reverend and Mrs. Mitchell Nolan. Small children, meanwhile, are not even acknowledged on the outer envelope, which is addressed to their parents; the inner envelope will have only the children's first names listed according to age under their parents' names.

Other rules to follow: titles are used in conjunction with first names on the outer envelope; the first names are dropped on the inner envelope. In the case of Miss Ann Thompson (addressed as such on the outer envelope), the inner envelope would read "Miss Thompson." In the case of an unmarried, cohabitating couple (or a same-sex couple), their names are listed in alphabetical order, like so: outer envelope—Mr. Mitchell Nolan, Miss Ann Thompson; inner envelope—Mr. Nolan, Miss Thompson.

"And Guest"

The phrase "and Guest" stirs up more trouble than it should. Followers of rigid etiquette rules frown upon these two little words (as in "Mr. Mitchell Nolan and Guest"). The proper way to go about this is to find out the name of the guest's guest and to issue her a separate invitation. This requires an extraordinary amount of time and effort, especially if you don't know the primary guest very well in the first place. (Will you really feel comfortable calling a distant relative to ask whether he's dating anyone special—oh, and by the way, could you have her name and address?)

 Fact

Before you send one invitation to an entire family, make sure any children who are included are under eighteen; if they're older, they should each be sent their own invitation, even if their address is exactly the same as their parents'.

No one will fault you for tacking "and Guest" onto the names in the inner envelopes. It's done every day and is becoming more and more standard practice. It's very kind of you to let your guests invite their own guests to your daughter's wedding; leave it at that and move on.

Responses

MOBs and brides alike love to run to the mailbox and gather up the responses to the wedding invitations. Organize a checklist with the names of the invitees so that you'll be able to easily tally a final head count for the caterer. If a guest simply fails to respond, don't be shy about making a phone call. There's no need to be snippy with the errant invitee, though. It's possible that this person forgot all about sending the response card, or just didn't realize the etiquette surrounding it.

CHAPTER 11

Where and How to Save Money

*U*p until this point, this book has focused on some basic wedding planning issues: how to get organized, how to design a strategy for successful communications with all of the interested parties, and how to find the right dress and the right caterer. If money is no object, all of this will be a relative breeze for you. The MOB who is forced to pinch pennies, however, will emerge from the planning process feeling either exhausted or triumphant. The difference? Creativity.

The Ground Rules

You already know that when you're working with a budget, the bride and groom need to prioritize their needs (and because all they really need to get married is a marriage license and an officiant, they'll actually be prioritizing wants—no matter how badly the bride feels she needs a $4,000 gown, that's a want). Before doing anything else, make a list of what's most important to the two of them. Include both the bride and the groom in this discussion so that you won't later be accused of being insensitive to your future son-in-law's wishes. Present them with the total budget, so that they both have some idea of how much money is in the wedding plan. If neither of them has previously demonstrated any understanding of the value of a dollar, this may be a great learning experience for them—both for the wedding planning and for the real life that follows.

Picking Favorites

Once their top choices have been laid out, the bride and groom have the option to try to include the less important items or vendors, or to leave them out altogether. You should encourage them to make wise choices here without taking over the list yourself.

For example, if your daughter has talked about nothing but the flowers since she got engaged and is willing to cut back on everything else in the name of dispersing blossoms and buds all over the church and reception area (where very little food will be served, by the way, because all of the money went to the decorations), encourage her to rethink this decision.

 **Essential**

Remember: your guests' comfort (i.e., food and drink) should be taken into consideration when planning the wedding budget, or else they shouldn't be invited. Lovely decorations and the best music are small comforts to people who are searching in vain for *anything* edible during the reception.

Give Yourself the Gift of Time

Every item on the list is fair game for creative price cuts. Be forewarned: This cost cutting is a commitment. This is not something that can be successfully achieved over a three-day period. But it's possible to pull off a classy, relatively inexpensive wedding if you get to work on the planning early enough. Getting a late start almost guarantees that you're going to pay too much for something, or that the final event will look shoddy.

Even if your daughter is planning a long engagement (a year and a half or more), don't give in to the urge to procrastinate (even if this is a primal urge for you). Don't tell yourself, "I work best under pressure," and don't allow yourself to believe that the most creative parties just happen without being planned. You may have planned hundreds of parties in your home this way, and all of them may have gone off without a hitch. Wedding planning is a completely different undertaking. You need to get with the program early on, especially if you're looking to save some money.

Stay Flexible

You and your daughter may have some very definite visions for her wedding. When you're looking to cut costs, it's all right to maintain those visions, but it's just as important to be flexible and open-minded. A florist may have some incredibly creative, low-cost ideas to present to the two of you, but if you go into that shop thinking, "Nosegays. Nothing but nosegays," you're severely limiting any assistance that can be rendered to you.

 Alert

> Be willing to listen to a vendor's ideas. If you're unwilling to bend, you'll end up getting exactly what you wanted, but you won't have saved a dime. Who knows, the alternate suggestion may have been the less expensive *and* more beautiful option.

When you're trying to save money on a wedding, ask for help from the experts, and listen to their suggestions. People who work in the wedding industry are usually accustomed to dealing with different-sized budgets. They know the current trends and also often know how to fake those trends using less expensive materials. Remember, these professionals answer wedding-related questions on a daily basis; don't be afraid to ask for their help. They won't think you're the cheapest person on the planet—they'll think you're just like the last MOB who walked through their doors.

Flower Power

It's no secret to anyone who's ever purchased flowers as a gift for someone else or anyone who loves to decorate their home with fresh flowers that they're expensive. You'd like to think that buying in bulk—say, for a wedding—would cut down on the cost of the little buds, but you'll find that the size of your bank account is the only thing reduced by purchasing yards of roses and lilies. Are you simply doomed, then, to spend more than you'd like on this aspect of your daughter's big day? No, ma'am. There are many ways to ensure that your daughter's wedding is beautifully decorated without diving headfirst into debt.

Finding the Florist

Start shopping around for the right florist as soon as you can. You'll want to compare services, creativity, and prices of various florists. Give yourself ample opportunity to see a floral designer's work at local weddings, receptions, or other events.

When you make an appointment to meet with the florist, have a solid concept of what you're willing to spend. A creative florist will have ideas for any budget; indeed, most florists can correctly be called artists. A florist who is in the business primarily to gouge customers will show you arrangements that are obviously above and beyond your means, and in that case, you should take your business elsewhere. This person is wasting your time in the hopes of pushing you to spend more. Another florist—one who will actually listen to what you're saying—is waiting for you. You just have to find him or her. Be persistent. (This is when you'll be glad you gave yourself plenty of time.)

DIY and Wholesalers

One popular suggestion for saving money on wedding flowers is to use silk flowers and try to make bouquets on your own (DIY style). If silk flowers are done well, they can look real; however, there's an overabundance of fake-looking silk out there, so you do have to choose carefully, and it's best not to enter into this project alone. Take a brutally honest friend or relative along on the silk-flower hunt. If she tells you she's never seen a blue daisy in all of her life, and incorporating the silk variety of this flower into your daughter's wedding will be tacky, listen to her. Also, for great quality silk flowers, you will find higher prices. You may find that buying all of the materials necessary for silk floral design might end up being the same cost as fresh flowers. Also, if you are not particularly crafty, you may end up hating the way the bouquets look after you have spent all that money. So tread lightly in the silk flower section at the craft store!

Some wholesalers will sometimes offer the same services as an independent florist (arrangements, delivery, wiring, or taping the bouquets) or be able to recommend a local florist in your price range. Internet companies can offer low prices on their products along with how-to instructions for assembling the floral arrangements for the wedding. If you're fairly confident that you can handle the care and delivery of the flowers (to the church and to the reception site) on the day of the wedding, this may be a viable option for you. Look carefully at the site's delivery policy. When will the flowers arrive, and how? Is there a contingency plan in case the truck or plane carrying your order doesn't arrive? You don't want to be left searching for flowers—any flowers—on your way to the church. Keep in mind that you will have a lot of work to do the day of the wedding and the day before. So before you say yes to DIY floral design, make sure you have ample help for this feat!

 Essential

Think about a compromise. If your daughter just has to have that fresh-flower smell at her wedding, have a mixture of real flowers where they're most important (in the bouquets and in the centerpieces) and silk flowers (or other less expensive options) where fresh flowers won't be missed.

Common Sense

When the bride is sighing over the gorgeous orchids in the flower shop, pull her away to look at something else—anything else, in fact. Some orchids tend to be among the most expensive floral options. Steer her toward flowers that are locally produced and widely available in your area. While almost any flower can be made available for a wedding, exotic blooms will cost you much more. If your daughter is getting married in December, wouldn't it be lovely and appropriate to incorporate poinsettias or amaryllis in the overall floral design instead of trying to dredge up some sunflowers?

Christmas and Easter are wonderful times for saving money on wedding flowers, because most churches are already decorated for these seasons. Valentine's Day, conversely, is one of the most expensive holidays to get married on or around; flower prices are routinely increased in the weeks preceding February 14.

More tips for saving money on the flowers:

- The bride can cut her number of attendants. Having ten bridesmaids means that she will need to shell out for ten bouquets (and most likely ten boutonnieres).
- A single flower with a ribbon is a simple way to cut costs for the bridesmaids.
- A wedding in an already decorated setting (think public garden or museum) needs very little in the way of decorations for the ceremony.
- Grocery-store florists are usually much cheaper than their independent counterparts. Be prepared to really investigate this option, though, to make sure the flowers are of the best quality.
- Splitting the cost of the church flowers can save you a bundle: Ask the minister if another wedding is scheduled for the same day, and contact the other bride.

And just remember what some men love to tell their significant others: Flowers die. Of course, these men are also likely to follow that phrase with, "No use spending good money on them." That sentiment doesn't exactly hold true here. A wedding might end up looking a little sad without a few blossoms to perk things up. However, you could wind up feeling downright morose if you discover too late that you could have spent much, much less on the decorations. Give yourself plenty of time and explore all of your floral options.

Dressing Up the Reception

If the reception is being held in a location without a single decoration, you could conceivably spend a fortune on simply making the place look less barren. A great option for dressing up plain halls is to call some local nurseries and ask them if they rent out potted plants. Put them in the corners, place them in the entryway, and pop one next to the head table. If you're not completely sold on this idea, thinking that everything will just look too green and dark, consider stringing some clear "twinkle" lights on the plants. There's just something dreamy and whimsical about little lights that echo stars in the sky or fireflies in the yard.

Candles are another less expensive option for beautifying a reception hall for less money. You'll find candles come in all sizes and colors, and are much cheaper than floral centerpieces. Float candles in various-sized cylindrical glass vases, or place pillar candles at different heights surrounded by votives for a romantic feel. You can also do different centerpieces at different tables. Have fresh flowers at half and candles at the other half to save some money. Make sure to ask your banquet manager if the use of candles is permitted in the facility. Hurricane lamps and cylindrical glass vases are often an option if the flames must be enclosed in glass.

 Fact

> Some brides opt for simple, fresh floral centerpieces and are still able to meet their budget. Consider a cluster of small bud vases at each table, or candles surrounded by fresh petals.

The Dresses

While the bride should be encouraged to take pity on her attendants and choose a dress that each of them can actually afford, in the end, this is not really your problem. Neither you nor the bride will be responsible for the cost of the bridesmaids' dresses. You'll be looking for your own dress and helping the bride to find her best look. Some brides (and MOBs) opt to put their dress near the top of their financial priority list, thinking that they'll be on display all day and that they only get to buy this kind of dress once. While this may be true, there are ways to dress to kill without emptying your wallet in the process.

Take Your Time

Starting early is going to make things much easier on you when you're looking for your own dress, and it's going to give the bride lots of time to mull things over when she's looking for hers. If she decides to order through a dress shop, she'll need to do so at least six months prior to the wedding, so the sooner she gets moving on the search for the perfect wedding fashion statement, the better.

Encourage her to explore all avenues before she decides on a dress. If she's dead set against buying a gown through a bridal store, she should start looking for a dress as soon as the ring hits her finger. Sure, it takes less time to purchase an off-the-rack dress from a boutique or department store, but if she doesn't find anything there, and she's only started looking a couple of months before the wedding, she's going to be in trouble.

Hunting for Bargains

Obviously, buying a gown at a bridal warehouse is going to be cheaper than buying that same dress through a bridal shop; that's why prospective brides place themselves in the middle of the competitive atmospheres that are a part of these shops. One word of advice you should offer to her: cheap is good; flattering is mandatory. She might snag a designer dress at a rock-bottom price, but if it doesn't look good on her, the money she's spent on it is a waste. No one will be reading the tag of her dress, after all, or be gossiping about the designer of the gown; guests will either be in awe of the bride's beauty (if she has chosen a complementary dress) or confused as to why she chose a gown that doesn't suit her at all.

If she'd rather not slog her way through the racks in the warehouses, she might opt to visit the local bridal shops. Are there bargains to be found here, or should the two of you resign yourselves to paying full price for any dress within the confines of those walls? You could get lucky and find a real deal, but you may also have to ask for the specials. Bridal stores run end-of-season discount sales; sometimes they have off-the-rack sample gowns for sale. Sales are usually advertised; the leftovers from these sales may sit until someone specifically comes looking for them.

 Essential

> The bride who's looking to save a buck on her dress may want to start by asking a friend or relative if she can borrow her old wedding gown. Most women have their dresses stored away somewhere and would be honored to be of assistance in this manner.

A bride who is looking for something a little less formal might find the perfect dress in the bridesmaids' racks. Some of these dresses are very elegant and are available in ivory, at much lower prices than the typical wedding dress. If your daughter is pursuing this option, she should also take a look in department stores and boutiques for evening gowns that could double as wedding wear.

Here Comes the Dress . . . Again

While many brides insist on having the dress of their dreams to have and to hold (in a box in their closet) from this day forward, others see the logic in spending far less for the dress they'll wear for one day and then pack away. These brides don't even care if their dress is brand new, which opens up another world of opportunity for them.

Bridal consignment shops specialize in recycling wedding dresses. If your daughter is in the market for a used dress, she can pop into one of these stores and browse around. If there's nothing to her liking (or nothing that fits), the storeowner can keep her eyes peeled for something that meets the description your daughter has given her.

Rental shops are one way to really keep costs low. Some bridal shops offer rental gowns, while some shops send their older gowns out to be rented. If you and the bride are dealing with a bridal shop but are thinking about renting, ask the owner about these other options.

 **Question**

What about saving money on the mother of the bride's dress?

Your options are very similar to the bride's. Start early and keep an open mind. Ask for discounts. Look for sales. Ask your friends about borrowing their MOB dress. Consider renting. Above all, make sure you look stunning in whatever you choose.

Renting a gown has its disadvantages, however. The bride will be choosing from a smaller selection of dresses (which is also one disadvantage to shopping in consignment stores); also, many shops won't do extensive alterations on their rental dresses, so the gown may not fit her as well as a purchased dress would.

There are also websites where brides sell their once-used dresses for a fraction of the cost. In most cases, the seller will allow the purchaser to return the dress if it is too small or too large for alterations. Many of these dresses are practically new and in mint condition. Here are some of the top websites where you can buy used wedding gowns:

- Tradesy—*www.tradesy.com/weddings*
- PreOwnedWeddingDresses.com—*www.preowned weddingdresses.com*
- Once Wed—*www.oncewed.com*
- Bravo Bride—*www.bravobride.com*
- Weddingbee—*www.weddingbee.com*

The Bar Tab

Prepare yourself: The bar bill for the reception can end up being astronomical. The very thought of paying top dollar for liquor sends some wedding sponsors into a mode of stinginess unparalleled by even the most stringent bean counters. Should you opt for a cash bar instead, or make it a "dry" reception? Rest assured, there are some ways to provide your guests with alcohol without going broke.

Cash Bar or Open Bar?

First things first: if you're inviting adult guests to a wedding, you need to provide them with food and drink. This means you have to shell out for some kind of alcohol. It's rude to ask your friends and relatives to attend the ceremony, bring a gift to the reception . . . oh, and pay for their own beer or wine or martinis, too. Unless the consumption of alcohol is against your religious or moral beliefs, accept the fact that you're going to have to face the bar bill. That being said, you don't have to make an open bar an extravagant, bank-breaking free-for-all. There are plenty of ways to open the bar on a fairly limited basis while still maintaining the appearance of being extremely generous to your guests.

Early Birds

If you're still in the earliest planning phases and the bride hasn't yet reserved the church or the reception hall, one of the best ways to cut back on the consumption of alcohol during the reception is to time it correctly. Think about it: When do most people start drinking? With dinner or in the early evening. Move the ceremony to the morning; follow it with a reception brunch or an early-afternoon lunch. During a brunch, you'll still want to include a champagne or sparkling-wine toast (or perhaps substitute mimosas, a.k.a., champagne diluted with orange juice); for an early-afternoon affair, you may want to include wine and beer in the open bar, or you might be able to substitute a champagne punch, which will lower your liquor cost substantially.

Cut It Back

If the bride has her little heart set on an evening reception, all hope is not lost. You can still control the amount (and type) of alcohol flowing from the bar into your guests' bloodstreams, but you'll need to know what's permitted in the reception hall and what isn't. Some ideas for your consideration (and to present to the banquet manager):

- **Tray service.** Have the servers carry trays of champagne and wine for a limited time. You're providing the guests with booze, but not for the entire evening. Expect to see fewer drunken guests than you would with a completely open bar.
- **Limit the drinks.** Offer beer, wine, and a cocktail matching the wedding's colors. The bridesmaids are wearing blue? Blue Hawaiians should hit the spot.
- **Nix the champagne toast.** Very few people actually choose to drink champagne. Have the guests toast the bride and groom with whatever they happen to be drinking at the time, or substitute a less expensive sparkling wine for an "official" toast.

Keep in mind that many upscale reception facilities charge an enormous markup on liquor, so don't be shy about asking if you can supply your own alcohol. You'll probably be charged a corkage fee, but you can bet that it will be less than paying for an open bar on the premises. In some cases, the corkage fee can be whittled down anyway.

Case by Case (by Case)

In the event that you are permitted to bring your own liquor to the reception, you'll need to know how much booze to buy. This may seem like a difficult task, but you can come pretty darn close to the right amount. Figure that each adult guest (here's where you go through the guest list and subtract any children from your head count—for now) will average four to five drinks over the course of an evening reception (some will drink more, of course, but some won't drink at all).

 **Essential**

Ask your liquor store about its return policy. You may already have plans for any leftover liquor, but if it's going to go to waste (or sit in your basement storage room forever), you might be able to return unopened bottles of wine and liquor.

From a fifth of alcohol (which, for you MOBs who don't spend a lot of time in the liquor store, is a fifth of a gallon, or about twenty-five ounces), you can serve up roughly 25 drinks using a one-ounce jigger to measure the liquor. Twelve bottles of liquor come in a case, so, using the one-ounce jigger to carefully dole out your alcohol, you can expect to serve up about 300 drinks from one case. (If you know your family likes their doubles, you'll obviously need to figure this into your equation.) One bottle of champagne or wine, meanwhile, will give you about 7 drinks.

A half keg of beer will provide the crowd with 260 eight-ounce glasses. Buying beer in a case? You'll need seven of them to equal a half-keg. And don't forget, you'll also need to stock the bar with nonalcoholic options and mixers for the liquor, not to mention lemons, limes, or anything else those drinks need for their finishing touches.

The Invitations

When looking for less expensive invitation options, you'll need to really get a handle on the process and the products. You'll want to know about paper weights (vellum? parchment? regular card stock?), printing methods, and all of the available options (panel cards, panel folders, overlays). The Internet is loaded with discount invitation vendors; however, if your order contains the lightweight, flimsy cards when the bride really wanted the heavy, stiff paper, you could witness the power of bridal drama at its absolute worst. It's fine to place your order with an Internet company (after you've carefully checked it out through the Better Business Bureau, of course)—just make sure you know what you're getting.

 Alert

Research is your best bet when ordering anything online. Thoroughly investigate the details of invitations before you place an order. Visit some stationery stores to look through their catalogs, and compare those products and services with what's available online.

Regarding the differences between printing methods, from a pricing standpoint, thermography is cheaper than engraving, and computer-printing programs are less expensive than hiring a calligrapher. Generally speaking, the more you add to invitations (more folds! more scrolls! more words!), the more expensive they're going to be. Purchasing inserts (reception cards, RSVP cards, pew cards, etc.) will also add to the final bill. While it's a nice touch to include these cards, you can absolutely print the information on the invitations and save yourself some dough.

The old adage "Less is more" rings true here. Your daughter can keep costs down by issuing lovely, simple invitations (not to say that plain-looking invitations are always the least expensive way to go—it all depends on the paper and the printing methods you've chosen). If the bride and groom (or you) are handy with a home printer—and have lots of time to practice—invitations can be handmade. Home printers are also an inexpensive option for printing out ceremony programs. Start early, invest in the appropriate software, and let your creative instincts take over!

Going Green

Incorporating eco-friendly elements can really help save money on your daughter's wedding. Of course, buying the pre-owned dress is a green way to go, but here are some other simple ways to save some green by going green:

- **Nix favors**—It is way greener to not have extra wedding "stuff" on the wedding day, so save some money and forgo getting favors.
- **Have a daytime wedding**—When you have a daytime wedding, you will inevitably save money and be green at the same time. Your guests will consume less food and alcohol and you will use less electricity (especially if the event is outdoors).

- **Have a vegetarian wedding**—This may sound crazy if you are not vegetarian. However, it is way cheaper to have a vegetarian menu and greener as well. You will be surprised by how certain caterers can really come up with delicious and interesting ideas for vegetarian and vegan fare.
- **Suit up the guys**—Instead of renting expensive tuxes, have the groom, groomsmen, and fathers wear suits they already own. If they don't own suits, buying a suit is still greener as they will be able to use the suit again after the wedding.

For every part of your wedding day, you can go green and save money. Ask your various wedding professionals about how they are using green policies to help save money and the environment.

Other Ways to Save

There are many other ways to save for a wedding, depending on your daughter's desires. The trick is to think about ways you can reuse items from the wedding and take an inventory of what you own and who you know.

Clothing

Since weddings are becoming more and more like stylized fashion shoots, some brides are opting for less formal wedding dresses. However, don't berate your daughter if she has decided to wear the "cutest cocktail dress she has ever seen"—one she knows she will wear again. Weddings are not considered "conventions of social etiquette" anymore, but rather expressions of the couple and their lifestyles. Don't force her groom to wear a rented tux when he is truly dashing enough in a fantastic navy suit (that he will use again). Both the bride and groom may opt for conventional wedding clothing but go for super-interesting shoes that they can wear again and again!

Nonprofits

You will be surprised when you dig deep into the information of some nonprofit organizations. You will find that they not only have interesting spaces to rent, but some of the rental fees for their buildings are actually tax-deductible. Be sure to take a look at local museums, galleries, animal sanctuaries, and parks. With interesting artwork and motivated staff, you might even find the service to be better at some of these facilities. A bonus is that you'll be giving back to the community while enjoying your daughter's wedding day.

Call in the Troops

Remember those potlucks and those fantastic yard sales you have put on with your neighbors? Why not ask some of the same people to help on the day of the wedding? If you just can't afford a wedding planner, ask a neighbor who loves to entertain to help out. Ask your friends about their local babysitters for taking care of the little ones. Ask about borrowing your brother-in-law's BMW to drive your little girl to the ceremony. The list is endless. If saving money is a top priority, take stock in the people you have in your life who can help save while making your daughter's day extra special.

Money Savers

Here is a list of simple but effective ways to save money:

- **Dessert**—Nix the fancy wedding cake and go for a different dessert bar. You can either have your caterer come up with something slightly less expensive or have a bake-a-thon with your family. Have your family bake up the traditional pie you always serve at Thanksgiving or the chocolate chip cookies you always used to make your daughter when she had a dance recital. Maybe your family is all about making candy. Dig out your family traditions in the dessert department and save hundreds of dollars.

- **Forgo the video**—While everyone loves an awesome video, go without the pricey videographer for the whole day. You can also contract a videographer to come only for the ceremony, or ask one person who will be at the ceremony close to the front to use the video function on their Digital SLR to save even more money.

- **Cocktail reception**—Instead of having a sit-down or buffet dinner, have a cocktail reception instead. Have the ceremony later in the evening with a small amount of food and a lot of dessert.

- **Brunch**—Having a brunch wedding will save you thousands of dollars if you do it right. First off, most people don't drink very heavily during the day. Second, brunch food is almost always cheaper than lunch or dinner food. Third, people don't dance as much during the day, so you won't have to shell out thousands for a band and you could possibly just have a sound system hooked up to your smartphone's music selections.

- **Go with a DJ**—Yes, a band is always fabulous at a wedding. However, a DJ is almost always going to cost less than a band.

- **No favors or gifts**—You don't have to give each of your guests a favor and you don't have to leave a hospitality gift in each hotel room. It is not 100 percent required, and the guests never miss them if one is not given.

- **Music**—As mentioned in the brunch option, you can create your own music playlist and just rent a sound system to play music at the reception. This is usually the best option for a casual wedding during the day that does not have a lot of announcements and heavy dancing going on.

- **Go veggie**—You may not be a vegetarian, but vegetarian weddings tend to be cheaper, as the cost of any meat and fish is higher than vegetables in general.

CHAPTER 12

Wedding-Day Overview

*N*o matter how long it seems to have taken to plan this wedding, you'll wake up one day—a date you will have burned into your memory forever—and realize that this is it. This is the day your daughter has been waiting for; this is the day you've put so much effort into; this is the one day you've been concentrating on for the past umpteen months. What should you expect from these last minutes, and how can you ensure smooth sailing?

Be Prepared

It's not unusual for the MOB to feel extremely stressed on the day of her daughter's wedding; in fact, you could start feeling tense in the weeks leading up to the big day, even if you're not a high-strung person in your regular life. What can you do to keep your cool? For starters, you need to take a realistic look at life in the final days and weeks prior to the wedding. More specifically, you need to make your own life easier during this time by not overscheduling yourself. Don't try to squeeze in a vacation two weeks before the wedding; don't agree to attend an out-of-town conference the week before; don't take on any big projects that will be due the day before the ceremony.

 Essential

Clear your schedule! You're going to be busy taking care of last-minute details and tying up any loose ends (and perhaps even repairing them) as the wedding draws near. You'll make yourself miserable if you take on too much too close to the wedding.

Once you've minimized your potential for overload, take a look at the outside world. Maybe it's been a while since you took the time to notice that, despite everyone's best intentions, life isn't perfect. You can't banish imperfection from the planet, not even for one day, not even if you plan every single detail. Don't expect the wedding day to be without its problems; in the end, you're dealing with humans—and humans make mistakes.

Just remember, you can greatly reduce the chance of anything going wrong by planning early and carefully, but you can never eliminate the potential for mishaps altogether. An MOB who can adapt and respond calmly to small problems is more likely to enjoy herself despite any last-minute changes in the overall wedding plans.

Communication

Although so much planning has been going on since day one (after the engagement), you have to make sure that you continue to keep an open line of communication with key players. Ask your daughter about the other things that are going on in her life. If you feel like she is being pulled in too many directions, ask the maid of honor to help when you know you can't. That is the maid of honor's job! Don't forget the groom. Although they are getting married, your daughter may be trying to hide her stress from her fiancé. Gently nudge your daughter to lean on him now—it's great practice for marriage.

Pre-Wedding Preparations

Whether the ceremony is scheduled for ten in the morning or five in the evening, there will be hustling and bustling before the big event. You and the bride will want to have your hair done and your makeup applied, the bridesmaids will arrive with excitement, and the men in your home will either flee or hang around trying to be helpful until you tell them it's time to get dressed for the ceremony. This is your moment to shine, Mom!

Hair Today

Depending on the length of her hair and the look she's going for, the bride may be able to do her own hair, or she may want a professional to handle the job for the ceremony. (It's advisable for most brides to leave their dos to someone who won't be a bundle of nerves on this particular day.) You'll probably want your hair done, too, so you'll either make an appointment for the same time as the bride (and perhaps the bridesmaids), or you might want to hire a stylist to come to the house. Obviously, the latter option is going to be more expensive.

 Alert

Every bride wants to look her absolute best for the pictures. Schedule hair appointments well in advance of the photographer's arrival to allow for any unforeseen, time-consuming adjustments to the bride's style (or anyone else's).

Advise the bride to start working with her hairstylist at least four months before the wedding to try different hairdos. She should keep the style of her headpiece in mind, and she should take it along so the stylist can get a good idea of how the bride's hair needs to look. If the bride is going to the hair salon on the day of the wedding, she should absolutely bring her veil, and she should wear a shirt with buttons down the front, so that she won't risk ruining her hair while dressing for her wedding.

You should keep the appearance of your dress in mind when choosing your own hairstyle for the wedding. If you're wearing a formal dress, have your hair done for the day. Nothing looks more peculiar than a head of casual hair atop a killer dress. If you took the time to find a gorgeous gown, complete your appearance with an appropriate hairstyle.

Put on a Happy Face

Makeup is sometimes an afterthought for brides and MOBs, and understandably so. After all, most women have been dealing with makeup for many years and have a day-to-day makeup routine (which may include no makeup at all) that can vary according to the time of day or a particular event. They don't see the need to bring in a cosmetologist for a wedding.

Maybe you know what looks best on you. Maybe you're almost a pro yourself. Just keep in mind that you and your daughter are going to be kissing people all day long; you're going to be rushing somewhere every minute of the day; you're going to be photographed over and over and over. However, this is a very special occasion. Go ahead and treat yourself to a professional beauty workup.

Start looking for a makeup artist several months before the wedding. If you don't know of any, ask your hairdresser if she can recommend someone. It's important for you to find someone who will get a sense of who you are; you don't want to end up looking like a showgirl if you're the more conservative type (or vice versa). You can also hit the cosmetics departments in the mall for free makeovers. If you like the products, buy them; if they don't look right on you at home, go back and ask how to apply them. Don't be pressured into buying products that aren't flattering, though, or that you know you won't use.

Flowers? Check!

The wedding day is a hurricane of activity: It starts first thing in the morning and doesn't end until the reception winds down. If you're not a wedding planner in your professional life (i.e., you don't deal with brides and bridesmaids and vendors on a weekly basis), you could find yourself feeling as though you've forgotten something and not realizing what it is until you arrive in church without your corsage. One way to minimize the possibility of this happening? Make a list—and check it many, many times.

The List

Dealing with multiple vendors can be a head-spinning experience. You'll need to touch base with each of them in the weeks prior to the wedding to confirm your order. (Do this even if you've already been assured that everything will be as promised. The MOB who keeps vendors on their toes has every right to complain if things go wrong.) It's in your best interest to start assembling a list of vendors and services at least a week prior to the wedding. The list should include:

- **Flowers:** How many of each type (bouquets, corsages, boutonnieres, baskets for flower girls, the bride's bouquet, arrangements for the church and/or reception), which extras (any accessories for the ring bearer, runner for the aisle), what time they should be delivered, and to which location.
- **Transportation:** How many limos have you hired? What color? What style? What time are they arriving? If you've hired a luxury car instead, you'll need the same information at your fingertips.
- **Ceremony programs:** Are they at the church or on their way? Who's in charge of them?
- **The photographer and/or videographer:** When will they be arriving at the house? Any special instructions?
- **Musicians:** When will they set up for the ceremony? For the reception?
- **The cake:** What time will the bakers arrive to assemble the confection at the reception site?
- **Reception:** Which appetizers should be laid out for the cocktail hour? What's for dinner? You need to have a grasp on these details on the off chance that something is missing or just isn't right.

Obviously, if there's another area of concern specific to your situation (someone needs to pick up Uncle Al at the airport, for example), this should go on your list as well. Keep a separate folder containing contracts and phone numbers within easy reach—just in case.

Help!

Now, you can make all the lists you want—you might be a champ at whipping them off, in fact—but you can't be in three places at once. You'll probably need to enlist help at some point, just to cover all of your bases. Don't try to simultaneously deal with the photographer and the florist when they both arrive at your house at the same time. Don't attempt to count baskets of flowers in the church while you're handing out ceremony programs.

 Essential

> Be sure to keep an eye on the clock. If the flowers are supposed to arrive at noon, call that florist if they aren't in your home by ten past. Know when things should be happening, and do your best to keep everything—and everyone—on track.

Handle the larger chores yourself, but recruit a friend or a family member to help with some of the smaller tasks. Let someone else dole out the programs at the door of the church. Trust your husband to peek out the window and make sure that two black limos are in the driveway; he'll tell you if they're pink.

The photographer may want you to pose for some pictures with the bride before the ceremony, so you'll have to make sure that you're prepared when he's ready for you. Everything should be under control at that point, but you'll want to have someone on standby to help just in case phone calls need to be made or a last-minute run to the corner store is necessary.

Off to the Ceremony!

To your amazement, you will eventually leave your home and find yourself traveling to your daughter's wedding. You may ride with her, or she may be in a separate car. If the two of you are side by side, try not to overload her with a lot of details. She'll probably be feeling nervous, and any last-minute instructions ("Don't forget to smile," "Make sure you aren't slouching when you're kneeling," or "Remember to speak loudly") are bound to cause her more anxiety than she can comfortably handle. Don't torment her with the specifics of the wedding either. That's your job at this point.

Details, Details

The bride can't very well go traipsing through the church to make sure that everything is in its place prior to the ceremony, so this job will fall to you. Take a good look at the groomsmen: Were their boutonnieres put on correctly? Are they all ready to go, or does that guy need to straighten his tie?

Take a look at the church: Have the correct flowers been delivered? Are there flowers from the last wedding that clash horribly with the baskets you've paid for? (Get rid of them, pronto. They'll ruin the pictures.) Have the ushers seated the guests according to their affiliations (bride's side to the left; groom's to the right), or are they weighing down one side of the church with anyone who walks through the door? Not that you should reseat people, but you can instruct the ushers on how to seat guests going forward.

 Alert

You can see it now: Your daughter's going to *weep* through her vows. Just in case, have one of the ushers place a package of tissues near where she'll be standing for the ceremony. She can discreetly pull them out as needed.

Take a look at the bridesmaids; make sure they all have their bouquets in hand and that none have been left behind in the limo. Does the flower girl have her basket? Has she been properly instructed on where she's going and where she will sit? If the maid of honor has a huge lipstick smear on her cheek from a well-wisher's kiss, wipe it off for her. You want to make sure that the wedding pictures—and everyone in them—look as good as possible.

Your last duty before taking your seat is to check on the bride and to make sure she's all right. She will be, deep down, but she'll want to know that you care, so no matter how stressed-out you're feeling, be nice.

Calmly check these last-minute details. There's a difference between being an organized, concerned MOB and being an obsessive-compulsive control fiend. You can actually be of great help to the bride and to the attendants if you can stay in control of your own emotions; if you're rushing around, barking out orders, everyone will avoid you, and you won't be able to accomplish anything.

During the Ceremony

Once you've given the attendants the final once-over, and after you've checked on the bride, you'll be seated for the ceremony. The MOB is the last person to be escorted into the church before the march of the bridesmaids begins. If one of your sons is standing up for the groom, he might walk you to your seat; if not, you'll be seen safely to your pew by one of the ushers. If you and the bride's dad are married to each other, you'll sit together in the front row on the left-hand side of the church (as you enter from the rear).

 Fact

When the ceremony ends, the bride and groom exit first, followed by their attendants, and then their parents. Don't try to sneak out before the maid of honor parades past you. Wait your turn.

Unless they've been tapped by the bride to read during the ceremony or to bring up the gifts, the parents of the bride and groom usually watch the proceedings from their seats. You are not responsible for adjusting the bride's dress or veil during the ceremony, nor should you step up to grab her bouquet while the couple exchanges rings. These tasks fall to the maid of honor, and she knows what to do. Don't embarrass her by whispering loudly to her as she passes you, "Don't forget to poof the train!" Sit back and enjoy the beauty of this event, which you worked so hard to help create.

The Interim

Depending on the time of the ceremony and the time the reception is set to begin, you may have several hours to fill between the two events. The bride and groom may be completely out of sight during this time, but that doesn't mean that you can take a break—your family and friends are all dying to talk to you, and you have plenty of time to spare before the reception. What should you expect to be doing during the interim, and how can you help your out-of-town guests pass the time?

Post-Ceremony Photography

The entire wedding party will probably be whisked off by the photographer for scores of pictures immediately following the ceremony. Usually, this photo shoot takes about an hour, but if they're traveling to a special site, they could be gone much longer than that (and if there are several hours between the wedding and the reception, it doesn't really matter). You shouldn't expect to go with them. Sometimes the photographer will take some family photos at the ceremony site immediately following the nuptials, but usually, this time is reserved for the bridal party to be photographed. You may see them before the reception, or you may not see them until you arrive at the banquet hall.

Out-of-Towners

When a wedding is scheduled for one o'clock and is being followed by an evening reception, a collective groan can sometimes be heard from the out-of-town visitors (this includes cross-country travelers as well as those who have made more than a thirty-minute drive to the ceremony). "What are we going to do to pass the time?" they wonder.

You may want to consider hosting an interim get-together at home for some of these people. Consider including the following people:

- Guests who were nice enough to make the drive across several towns to attend the ceremony and who don't necessarily want to spend the day driving back home and then traveling back again for the reception
- Friends and family who have spent a considerable amount of time and money traveling across several states to wish the bride and groom well
- Guests who may live nearby but whom you see rarely

Many guests, you will notice, will choose to skip the ceremony when there's a several-hour delay between the vows and the reception. Anyone who has cleared his or her entire day to attend the church service and the reception would like to know that you appreciate the effort. Inviting these folks back to your home for a casual gathering is a great way to show your appreciation. This does not have to be a formal affair. A few deli trays and some pastries will be enough to hold over even the hungriest guests. Make sure you have enough seats for everyone, especially if the bridal party will be stopping in after the photographer has finished with them.

Keep Them Busy

If you can't host an interim party for whatever reason, make sure you've given your guests the skinny on the area: Let them know if there's something special happening in town during the wedding weekend, and be sure to mention points of interest, such as museums, parks, or shops. Include this information when you send their invitations. While you shouldn't try to stuff a brochure into the envelope, you might want to include some helpful websites along with a map of the area, highlighting any areas of interest.

Internet- and social media–savvy brides and grooms are finding that creating a wedding website is incredibly helpful for relaying pertinent information to their guests. If your daughter and her fiancé have set up their own site, ask them to send e-mails to friends and relatives who will be looking for some entertainment options during their stay.

The Reception

An MOB works so hard over the course of a wedding day, there should really be a great big payoff waiting for her somewhere. Wait a minute—there is! Your daughter's happiness and the knowledge that you were able to create a beautiful event is your reward. Not what you had in mind? There's another bonus: The reception is the time when you might finally be able to relax a little and really enjoy yourself . . . once you have approved the details, that is.

The Receiving Line

Some brides and grooms are choosing to forgo the receiving line these days, complaining that it takes them away from their own party and arguing that no guest really enjoys making their way through the never-ending lineup anyway. Bridesmaids and ushers are forced to make small talk, and the bride and groom find themselves kissing and hugging strangers.

 Alert

As the structure of the traditional family is changing, the receiving line is following suit (in other words, no one is going to force bitterly divorced parents to stand next to one another and smile). Let the bride and groom choose what works best for both families.

Your response? Too bad, kids. Anyone who comes to the wedding deserves to be personally greeted by the primary players, and there's simply no easier way to do this than by having a receiving line. Keep in mind that many of your older guests will expect this tradition, and may well feel snubbed if the bride and groom eliminate it. Imagine the response of your friends and relatives, who have made a great effort to attend this event, when they realize that the newlyweds don't want to be bothered with welcoming them—they'd rather be having fun. Tell the bride and groom there will be plenty of time for play once they've said hello to every single guest.

The receiving line does not have to include all of the attendants. By cutting the size of the line, you'll also cut down the time it takes for your guests to navigate it as well as the amount of time the bride and groom will have to miss their party. The bride and groom can greet the guests by themselves, or they might want to include their parents, or only the mothers (while the fathers spend their time mingling with the guests during the cocktail hour). All of these options are perfectly acceptable.

Other Options?

There are alternatives to the receiving line, but most are fairly time-consuming and don't allow your guests the opportunity to kiss the newlyweds. One option is for the bride and groom to stop and greet the rows of guests as they leave the church. This is a good way for the bride and groom to give a quick wave and a smile to everyone in attendance. On the other hand, it's not as personal as a face-to-face greeting, and it could create a bottleneck in church. (No one wants that, especially on a hot summer day.) The bride and groom might also opt to swing by each table during dinner to say hello to their guests. This is a nice touch in addition to the receiving line, but again, it's fairly impersonal and probably not what the diehard receiving-line advocates will find acceptable.

Be on Guard!

The cocktail hour will include drinks and hors d'oeuvres, socializing, and a bevy of guests asking you where the gift table is. Most reception facilities will set up an area that's somewhat out of the way so that guests aren't constantly tripping over gifts, but it shouldn't be so hidden that someone could rifle through the goodies without notice. Assign a friend or relative to keep an eye on the bride's bounty.

 **Question**

Is it really necessary to have someone guard the gift table?

No one *you* know would steal a present, but any stranger could waltz in off the street and make off with a package or two. This is especially true of envelopes containing cash, so make sure that the gift table is in plain sight and guarded.

Your official duties at the reception are to be the hostess and to make sure everything goes according to plan. Again, there's being organized and assertive, and then there's crossing the line into being a little controlling and nutty. Nutty MOBs don't get anywhere with vendors if and when problems occur; cool-headed, well-spoken, well-informed MOBs do.

You and the bride will have discussed how the DJ or bandleader will introduce the wedding party. Expect to be heralded by the crowd when your name is announced.

You'll take your seat and enjoy the fabulous dinner you and the bride have so carefully selected.

Order of Events

The cocktail hour is first, followed by dinner, if you've chosen to serve a meal. Before anyone digs in, the best man traditionally offers a toast. The toasting doesn't need to stop there, though, and if your family loves to honor its members, you could find yourself listening to a long line of heartfelt speeches. If anyone would like to offer some kind words to the newlyweds, the traditional order of toasters is as follows: best man, groom's father, bride's dad, groom, bride, friends or relatives, maid of honor, groom's mother, MOB, and anyone else.

 Fact

Everyone loves good leftovers! Don't be afraid—and don't feel like a cheapskate—to ask to have any uneaten dinners wrapped to take home. You've already paid for them, and they'll end up in the garbage otherwise.

If something is amiss during dinner—the food is cold, or the service is lousy—find the banquet manager at once and make him aware of your concerns. Even if he can't fix something immediately, you need to give him the chance to rectify the situation; if he can't, you have every right to ask for a partial refund at the end of the evening. Reputable businesses will be very apologetic if something clearly isn't right, and will refund the price of a number of dinners. If you keep your complaints to yourself until the end of the reception, you may have far less leverage.

Once dinner has wrapped up, the dancing will start. The bride and groom share a dance, then the bride dances with her dad and the groom dances with his mom. This is followed by a dance for the parents of the newlyweds and then a song for the bride to dance with her father-in-law while you and the groom dance together. By this time, your guests could be yawning and ready to head home, and you'll be amazed when you realize that it's after ten o'clock. Combine some of these dances. They're very time-consuming, and you and the groom (or the bride and her new father-in-law) might feel very uncomfortable being in the spotlight together. Let the guests share the dance floor with the wedding party as soon as possible.

Toss It

The bouquet and garter toss is a tradition that has been around for ages; however, it has been falling out of favor because many see it as a sexist practice. If your daughter wants to skip this altogether, let her. She knows what the young women in the crowd will be comfortable with. If she fears none of them will play along with a young bachelor inching a garter up a random female leg, don't argue with her. She may still want to throw the bouquet, though, and that's perfectly fine.

A Post-Wedding Party

After the reception has ended, some families like to keep the party train moving. You might want to host a post-wedding party, especially if the reception will be wrapping up fairly early in the evening and you know your guests will be looking to revel some more. This can be an informal, at-home affair including only a small, select number of guests, or you might want to look into keeping the party going at the reception site after the newlyweds have hit the road. You can be sure that you'll end up with a larger number of guests if you choose the latter option, as there's no nice way to give anyone who's already in attendance the boot.

"Hostess with the Mostest"

If you are still concerned with proper wedding etiquette (and have not already done so), consider investing in an etiquette book. It is important that the MOB keeps up with proper social graces, so you need to be ready for your daughter's wedding—and be the "hostess with the mostest" all day long. Here are a few last-minute tips you should follow:

- Be sure you have the proper gratuity amounts ready with your handwritten notes.
- Have any gifts that have not been given to the wedding party in the back seat of your car to make sure they get them before they leave town.
- You must always remember (no matter how many of your family members are feuding among themselves or with you) to keep a smile on your face and to offer a hand to shake.

- Have a backup to your backup plan. That way, you will have other choices should problems arise. Think emergency kit, taxi-company numbers, an extra set of shoes, and anything else that will make you feel more comfortable on the day of the wedding.

Toasting Basics

You may not be the one toasting the bride and groom at the reception, but there are several reasons why the mother of the bride needs to know how to toast. The best man may start to sweat when he realizes he left his written speech in the hotel room. The maid of honor, asked by the bride to give a small toast, freezes up at the last second. The MOB is typically the one who everyone turns to in the case of a "toast" emergency. Why? You know everything about the bride, and know exactly what to say—with poise, passion, and grace. Follow these toasting basics:

- Remember that the focus of wedding toasts should be the bride and groom. Do not go into long litanies about your personal history with them.
- Most toasts are typically short. If a toast is done correctly, anything from two to three sentences to one minute's worth of talking is more than enough to convey a special message to the happy couple.
- Avoid inside jokes. Focus on one fantastic anecdote or one truth about the couple's love for each other.
- Always stand, raise your glass, and keep some level of eye contact with the bride and groom.

CHAPTER 13

The Best
Mother-in-Law Ever

*A*fter the wedding, life goes on. The newlyweds will be faced with piles of presents—and blank thank-you notes. They may drop out of sight or seem distant for a while. They could be looking for a home, and then they might realize that they haven't the slightest idea of how to take care of a house. The good MOB stands back and carefully considers what she's going to say about these issues before she says (or does) anything.

Thank-You Notes

Nothing is more upsetting to a mom who has just invited legions of friends and family to a wedding than a daughter who refuses to write thank-you notes for all of the gifts that have been lavished upon her and her new husband. Is this a generational gap? Is it standard practice for brides to thank guests in person for gifts, and let it go at that? No, it isn't. This is one issue that's worth harping on until you see the bride breaking down and penning her gratitude.

It's the Right Thing

No matter what assumption the bride and groom may have been under, a guest is never obligated to either attend a wedding or give a gift. Anyone who has bothered to bring (or send) the newlyweds a present deserves a handwritten note of appreciation. Be sure the bride and groom understand how important thank-you notes are.

 Essential

Since most registries are online way before the wedding, many gifts will start to arrive before the wedding. Have your daughter write thank-you notes as she receives the gifts, and then she can send them out after the wedding. There will be less work to do when she comes back from the honeymoon.

The note should be short and sincere, and should make some mention of the specific gift and its intended use. For example, if your cousin Martha sent the bride a tablecloth, the bride could write a note along the lines of the following:

Dear Martha,

Thank you so much for the beautiful lace tablecloth. Jim and I just love it, and will use it for our most formal dinners. It was so kind of you to think of us.

Love,

Mary

If Martha has sent the ugliest tablecloth you've ever seen, the note should still read the same. (It's the thought that counts.) Now, if Martha gave the newlyweds money, a thank-you note might read:

Dear Martha,

Thank you very much for the generous gift. Jim and I are looking for a new couch, and we'll use your money toward the purchase. It was great to see you at the wedding. I hope we'll see each other again soon.

Love,

Mary

Notice how there's no mention of the specific dollar amount, but the bride tells Martha exactly where that money is going to be used, which will give Martha a sense of having made a significant contribution that the kids really appreciate.

No Time to Waste

If the wedding was a large one, the bride and groom should start writing these notes as soon as they return from the honeymoon. The guests will also want to know that the bride and groom received their presents, and that nothing was lost in the shuffle.

When the bride and groom open the gifts, they should keep a list of who has given what, and refer to that list when writing their notes. No one wants to be thanked for the wrong gift.

Just Make Them Do It

Don't accept no for an answer here. While there are plenty of issues that are fair game for negotiation after the wedding, this isn't one of them. It's very impolite to invite guests to a party, take their gifts, and then not acknowledge them, especially in this situation.

 **Question**

Are thank-you notes the bride's responsibility, or should the groom help?
Of course, the groom should help out, especially if both of them are working full-time. Writing 100 or so thank-you notes is a time-consuming job; two pens working furiously will cut the time in half.

Since some of the guests are your friends and relatives who don't know your daughter from anyone else in the world, they came to the wedding at your request. If the bride wants to leave her own friends hanging, wondering whether she liked their presents, that's one thing (because it will affect their opinion of her); however, she shouldn't be allowed to do the same to the folks you invited (because it will affect their opinion of her and you).

The Newlyweds' Attitude

After you've settled the issue of the thank-you notes, you'll move on to more important life issues—such as why the bride and/or groom seem to be avoiding you. It's difficult for an MOB to switch gears so quickly, to go from being so involved in the wedding to adopting a hands-off attitude with the newlyweds. Realize that the months after the wedding are a crucial time for them. The bride and groom have to establish their own sense of identity as a married couple. The relationship you establish with them here and now is going to fore-shadow the years to come.

Hold Your Tongue

No one ever tells the bride and groom that learning to live together is always a piece of cake. The smallest problems can be worthy of award-winning dramatics from either newlywed, and brides are especially prone to telling their mothers far too much. Is your new son-in-law refusing to pull his weight around the house, leaving all the chores for your daughter? Is he hitting the bars with his single friends? Is he careless with money?

Obviously, any new wife would have a hard time dealing with some of these issues. It's likely that she wouldn't want to share her anxiety with a lot of people, and she may not trust anyone like she trusts you. This puts you in a tough spot. You're hearing the worst of it, but remember, you're not expected to pass judgment. In fact, even if the bride requests judgment, keep it to yourself.

What can you do here? Listen. If she wants advice, offer the most neutral, nonjudgmental guidance you can muster. Let her know that every newly married couple has issues to work through. Even when she's upset with him, her primary allegiance is to him. Criticizing him will only cause a rift between you and your son-in-law (because somehow, somewhere, your daughter will repeat your words to him), and that's sure to cause trouble between you and your daughter.

Back Off a Bit

Even if you are the least judgmental mom on the planet, you can still cross the line into meddling territory if you're simply around too much. Remember, the newlyweds need time to get used to living together—they need to get a feel for each other's daily rhythms, habits, and quirks. They need quiet time to sit and talk. They need to do things together, alone.

They're only going to be newlyweds once, and for a relatively short time. It won't be long before they fall into the routine of many long-term marriages, where one of them is working too much, and the other one is anxious to have visitors. They'll have kids of their own soon enough, and they'll need help with the babysitting and carting the tots around town to playdates and preschool. In other words, there will be plenty of time for you to be with them somewhere down the line. Don't crowd them in their first year of marriage, when every minute they spend together—no matter what the setting—is worthy of a romantic journal entry or an ardent poem. When they want company, they'll invite you to their home. Avoid popping in to surprise them.

 Fact

The newlyweds haven't moved to Mars. Chances are if you're living in the same area, they may want and *need* your assistance from time to time—with decorating, or with laying out a budget. No one is telling you that you can't see them. Just don't smother them.

Even if you are extremely close to your daughter, you have to give her and her new husband room to breathe after the wedding. Your exceptional relationship will very likely continue, as long as you don't put her in the awkward spot of having to avoid your phone calls and ignore your knocking at the front door so she can snag some private time with her hubby.

Traditional Hotspots

So now you know to never badmouth your son-in-law (or at least not while the kids are still settling into married life), and you know you need to give your daughter and her new husband plenty of space. You should also be aware of some of the other ways well-meaning mothers-in-law get themselves into hot water with one or both of the newlyweds. Stay away from these touchy subjects:

- **Suggesting upgrades to their home.** If your daughter has always been accustomed to having the best that money can buy, it may disturb you to see her living in newlywed pauperism. They won't be broke forever, and they will resent your implying that they should be fabulously wealthy right now.

- **Talking about the past.** Your daughter was seriously considering marrying another guy (or you were dreaming of their union), or you feel she gave up a career for her husband. Drop it. Dwelling on what might have been is a big waste of time for you, and incredibly irritating for everyone else.

- **Talking about the future.** Don't push your dreams onto the newlyweds. If she and her husband are talking about starting a family, and she's going to be staying home for a few years, don't push the topic of her finishing her PhD right now. (And don't push kids right away if she wants the PhD first.)

- **Blaming the son-in-law.** When a daughter makes a choice that is unwise (as far as her mother is concerned), it's common for Mom to look to the obvious source of the problem—her son-in-law. That's unfair. Your daughter has a mind of her own, you know.

There are countless variations of these topics, and numerous other issues, as well. You're thinking that this is unfair, and that you'll either resign yourself to a life of keeping your mouth shut or you'll be criticized for everything you say to your daughter and her husband. That's not exactly true. As time goes by, you'll learn what's acceptable to them and what isn't.

 Alert

> Don't criticize the groom's family. No matter how bad you or the bride might think they are, they're *still* his blood relatives. If you can't say something nice about them, try to forget they even exist.

You'll also learn to care about some things, and to forget others. You may not give a darn if your son-in-law gets angry with you for encouraging your daughter to take the full-time job she's considering; on the other hand, you may decide that what your daughter and her husband do for a living doesn't really affect your life, so . . . why should you lose sleep over their decisions?

Last but Not Least

Being a good mother-in-law is really an art form. It may come naturally to you, or it might take some effort. The important thing is that you realize that all relationships are constantly evolving, and if you aren't exactly wild about your son-in-law at one point in time, you could find that six months down the road, he seems like a completely new (and improved) man.

The bride and groom are maturing in their relationship right after the wedding, but many times, they're also struggling to mature in their own skins at the very same time. Technically, they're adults, but they feel like kids, and suddenly, they're coping with joint finances, in-laws, and everyday ups and downs. When your son-in-law is not exactly behaving like the Prince Charming you expected him to be, cut him a little slack. It could be that your daughter hasn't exactly been the ray of sunshine he was counting on.

Try to remember that your daughter has to learn how to be a wife now, too. You can help her when she asks; just be careful not to come between her and her new husband. Let them work through the first year before you start evaluating where their relationship is headed—and where you fit into the picture.

Planning Timeline

*P*lanning a large wedding takes time and organization. You'll need to know which vendors to contact and when, and you'll also need to make a little timeline for yourself to make sure that everything has been taken care of. The following timeline will give you a good overview of the whos, whats, and whens of wedding planning.

What to Do and When

Some brides opt for lengthy engagements because they know that their dream reception hall is booked solid eighteen months in advance. Other brides have less time to plan but manage to pull off a stunning event nonetheless (with the help of the MOB, of course). Regardless of the timing of the engagement, there are some things you and the bride should get started on as soon as possible. Other things can wait a bit. Use the following checklist as a guideline.

As Soon As Possible

Here is a list of things you should do as soon as your daughter gets engaged:

☐ Announce the engagement to the families.
☐ Start narrowing down dates and times for the ceremony and reception.
☐ Decide on the budget.
☐ Talk about how formal or informal, and how large or small, the wedding will be.
☐ Divide the guest list numbers and draw up preliminary lists.
☐ Ask friends and family for vendor recommendations.
☐ Purchase and prepare (by labeling them, for example) various organization supplies.
☐ Call the church; establish contact with the officiant.

❑ Book interviews with vendors. Start thinking about booking them if the wedding is only a year away—or earlier if you're positive you want a particular vendor.

Nine Months Prior to the Wedding

❑ Bride should select and contact bridesmaids.
❑ Start shopping for dresses (bride's and bridesmaids').

Six Months Prior

❑ Think about hosting an engagement party.
❑ Finalize the guest list.
❑ Review vendor options and finalize contracts.
❑ Book lodging for out-of-towners.
❑ Shop for your MOB dress and notify the groom's mom of the style and color.
❑ Start working with the hairstylist in order to find the best look for the wedding. Wedding-day appointments should be made.

Four Months Prior

❑ Order invitations.
❑ Send the engagement announcement to newspapers.
❑ Bride and groom register for gifts.
❑ Shower plans should be in the works.
❑ Plan seating charts for the reception.

Two Months to Six Weeks Prior

☐ Confirm the hotel room block for out-of-town guests.
☐ Mail the invitations.
☐ Have dress alterations made.
☐ Bride may have her portrait taken for newspaper wedding announcement.

Four Weeks Prior

☐ Finalize the seating charts as acceptances and regrets come in.
☐ Confirm menu choices with the caterer or reception hall.

One to Two Weeks Prior

☐ Contact guests who haven't responded to invitations.
☐ Give final head count to the caterer.
☐ Call and confirm dates and times with vendors.
☐ Start making your wedding-day checklist.
☐ Tie up any loose ends (make sure the bride has her undergarments and accessories; give your own ensemble the once-over; make sure your husband has actually been fitted for his tux).

One Day Prior

☐ Attend rehearsal and rehearsal dinner.
☐ Assign last-minute duties to friends and family members.
☐ Get a good night's sleep.

APPENDIX B

What Are You Saying? Invitation Wording

*I*t's time to order the invitations. Do you know what you want them to say? The following section includes options for wording even the most complicated invitations.

General Rules

In the following examples, note how almost everything is spelled out: the time, the date, the year. Very few abbreviations are permitted on formal invitations. (Mr. and Mrs. are among the few that are allowed.) Also note how the actual address of the church isn't given; the only time you would include the street number would be if the wedding were taking place in an area where leaving the address out would create confusion. For example, if your daughter is getting married in a huge city, you'll probably want to let the guests know which block of a particular street the church is located on. The rules for including the street number on the invitation follow the same guidelines as writing them in a publication: Any number under 100 is written out—as in Forty-Two East Avenue—anything over 100 can be numerically represented.

The Bride's Parents Are Hosts

If the bride's parents are the sole hosts of the wedding, the invitation will read as follows:

Mr. and Mrs. Elliot Hunt

request the honor of your presence

at the marriage of their daughter

Anne Marie

to

Mr. Jacob Thomas White

on Saturday, the first of June

Two thousand and thirteen

at one o'clock in the afternoon

Pine Ridge Methodist Church

Pine Ridge, New York

The Groom's Parents Are Hosts

Similarly, if the groom's parents are hosting, the invitation would say:

Mr. and Mrs. Andrew White

request the honor of your presence

at the marriage of

Miss Anne Marie Hunt

to their son

Mr. Jacob Thomas White . . .

Both Sets of Parents Are Hosts

If both the bride's and groom's parents are helping to sponsor the wedding, the invitation should say:

Mr. and Mrs. Elliot Hunt

and

Mr. and Mrs. Andrew White

request the honor of your presence

at the marriage of

their children

Anne Marie

and

Jacob Thomas

Mixed-Family Rules

When divorce and remarriage come into play, the wording is a little different.

The Mother of the Bride Is Hostess

Mrs. Elliot Hunt

requests the honor of your presence

at the marriage of her daughter . . .

This assumes the mother has not remarried and has kept her married name. If she has remarried, of course, she would use that name; if her new husband is also sponsoring the wedding, his name would be included as well, but the bride would be referred to as "her" daughter (not "their"), unless the bride has been adopted by her stepfather.

Parents and Stepparents Are Hosts

In the case of divorce and remarriage all around, with all of the parents cohosting, the invitation *could* read something like this:

Mr. and Mrs. Joshua Peters

[bride's mother, remarried]

and

Mr. and Mrs. Elliot Hunt

[bride's father, remarried]

along with

Mr. and Mrs. Carl Lucia

[groom's mother, remarried]

and

Mr. and Mrs. Andrew White

[groom's father, remarried]

request the honor of your presence

at the marriage of their children

Anne Marie Hunt

and

Jacob Thomas White . . .

Of course, in doing this, you've pushed the bride and groom way down to the bottom of the page and have made all of the remarriages the main issue instead of the wedding at hand. A better way to word an invitation like this is as follows:

Together with their parents,

Anne Marie Hunt

and

Jacob White

request the honor of your presence . . .

Bride and Groom Are Hosts

When the bride and groom host their own wedding, they would simply list their own names at the top of the invitation:

Anne Marie Hunt

and

Jacob White

request the honor of your presence

at their marriage

on Saturday, the first of June . . .

Or . . .

The honor of your presence is requested

at the marriage of

Anne Marie Hunt

and

Jacob White

on Saturday, the first of June . . .

Reception Cards

You'll also have to word the reception cards correctly. If the cards are being slipped into the wedding invitations to inform the guests of the location of the party following the ceremony, they can simply read:

Reception

at six o'clock in the evening

Pine Ridge Yacht Club

Pine Ridge, New York

The response cards would also be enclosed:

M_____

____ *accepts*

____ *regrets*

Or more to the point:

> *The favor of a reply is requested*
> *on or before the fifteenth of May*

M_____

_____ *will attend*

_____ *will not attend*

Index

Announcements, 17–21
Attire. *See also* Bridal gown
    accessorizing, 174–75
    costs of, 54, 63, 219
    formal attire, 162–63
    for mother of bride, 160–70,
      230
    renting, 230, 237–38
    rules on, 160–64
    shopping for, 164–77, 228–30

Bachelorette party, 157. *See also*
  Parties
Beauty salon, 73, 177, 244–45
Bouquet toss, 50
Bridal gown
    changing, 49
    cost of, 54, 63, 100–101, 219
    money-saving tips for, 100–101,
      227–31
    previously worn gown, 100–
      101, 229–31
    renting, 230
    selecting, 170–74
Bridal shops, 168–77, 228–30
Bridal shower, 148–53. *See also*
  Parties
Bride
    attire for, 54, 100–101, 170–74,
      229–31
    communicating with, 21–26, 86
    dreams of, 23–26
    planning wedding with, 12,
      21, 24
Bridesmaids, 84, 154–55
Brunches, 158–59, 232, 239–40
Budget. *See also* Expenses
    discussing, 25–26, 81–83,
      218–20

    money-saving tips, 218–40
    for wedding, 12–13, 25–26,
      56–64

Cakes, 40, 51, 105–7
Caterers, 71–72, 103–5
Ceremony. *See also* Wedding day
    arriving at, 249–51
    civil ceremony, 102
    cultural traditions for, 47–49
    family members in, 41
    nontraditional ceremony,
      92–93
    overview of, 241–61
    post-ceremony events, 252–54
    religious ceremony, 102
    seating for, 41, 251
    setting for, 101–2, 238
Children at wedding, 140, 195–96,
    204, 216–17
Chuppah ceremony, 47
Civil officiants, 41, 55, 72–73
Communication tips, 21–26, 39–40,
    86, 266–72
Cultural traditions, 46–49, 119

Dancing, 41, 259
Decorations, 72, 113–15, 222–27.
    See also Flowers
Delicate situations
    ex-family relations, 179–86,
      189–91
    family dynamics and, 178–93
    grandparents and, 192
    keeping peace in, 189–92
    same-sex weddings, 196–200
    second weddings, 193–96
    special roles and, 192–93

step-family relations and,
181–92
Destination weddings, 64–67
Drinks/beverages, 54, 71, 231–34

Engagement, announcing, 15–32
Engagement party. *See also* Parties
etiquette for, 27–30
expenses for, 53–54
guest list for, 29–30
hosting, 53–54
planning, 28–29
Entertainment, 110–13. *See also*
Musicians
Expenses
beauty salons, 73
budget for, 12–13, 25–26, 40,
56–64
caterers, 71
decorators, 72
for family of bride, 53–73
for family of groom, 40–41, 55
flowers, 40–41, 54–55, 72
food/drink, 54, 71
gifts, 41
gratuities, 71–73
money-saving tips, 218–40
musicians, 41, 54, 73
officiant fee, 41, 55, 72–73
photographers, 73
post-wedding expenses, 69–70
reception venue, 54, 71–72
rehearsal dinner, 40
responsibility for, 40–41, 52–73
traditional expenses, 12–13,
53–55
vendors, 54–55, 69, 71–73
videographers, 73

Facebook, 132–34
Family dynamics, 178–93
Family of groom

expenses for, 40–41, 55
financial responsibilities of,
40–41
friends with, 36–42
meeting, 33, 36–51
planning wedding with, 42–44,
85–86
rehearsal dinner and, 44–45
seating for, 41
Family traditions, 42, 45–51
Fashion blogs, 128–29
Father of bride, 81–83, 180–92
Father of groom, 258–59
Favors, 61, 101
Flowers
gratuity for, 72
money-saving tips for, 222–27
responsibility for, 40–41, 54–55
selecting, 113–15, 222–27,
246–48
Food/caterers, 54, 71–72, 103–5

Garlands/leis, 48–49
Garter toss, 50
Gifts
for attendants, 41, 54–55
for groom, 54
hospitality gifts, 60
at reception, 257, 260, 265
registry for, 78, 152, 263
thank-you notes for, 263–66
Google+, 137–38
Gratuities, 71–73. *See also* Vendors
Groom
family of, 33, 36–51, 55, 85–86
father of, 258–59
meeting, 34–36
mother of, 36–42, 55
Groom's cake, 40
Guest list
"B" list, 208–10
for both families, 44, 201–4

invitations and, 210–13
planning, 32, 201–6
for second wedding, 206–8
Guests
accommodations for, 116–18
comfort of, 59–60, 220
responsibility of, 66–67
social media and, 123–24
transportation for, 60–61, 101, 116

Health blogs, 127–28
Honeymoon, 55, 69, 263, 265

Instagram, 134–35
Invitations
addressing, 214–17
for children, 204, 216–17
costs of, 54
examples of, 277–83
mailing, 209, 214
money-saving tips for, 235–36
ordering, 213–14, 276–77
for post-wedding reception, 68
responses to, 217
rules for, 277
selecting, 210–13
wording for, 276–83

Jumping the broom, 47

Leis/garlands, 48–49
Luncheons, 154–57

Mandap ceremony, 47–48
Marriage license, 41, 219
Money matters. See also Expenses
budgets, 12–13, 25–26, 56–64
discussing, 23–26
responsibility for expenses, 40–41, 52–73
saving money, 218–40

Money-saving tips
assistance with, 218–20, 238–40
for bar tab, 231–34
for decorations, 222–26
for dresses, 227–31
for eco-friendly options, 236–37
for flower costs, 222–27
for invitations, 235–36
for nonprofit venues, 101, 238
planning ahead, 220–21
for reception, 231–34
for vendor costs, 219–23
Mother of bride
attire for, 160–70, 230
communicating with bride, 21–26, 86
duties of, 74–94
expectations of, 75–78
as mother-in-law, 262–71
responsibility for expenses, 53–73
role of, 11–13, 58, 75–77, 180–81
Mother of groom
communicating with, 39–40
friends with, 36–42
help from, 40
meeting, 36
responsibility for expenses, 40–41, 55
Musicians, 41–42, 73, 110–11

Newlyweds, 266–71
Nikah ceremony, 48
Nontraditional reception, 92–94. See also Reception
Nontraditional wedding, 92–95. See also Wedding

Officiant fee, 41, 55, 72–73
Organization tips, 30–32

Parties
    bachelorette party, 157
    bridal shower, 148–53
    brunches, 158–59, 232, 239–40
    engagement party, 27–30
    luncheons, 154–57
    planning, 141–59
    post-wedding parties, 67–68,
        158
    pre-wedding parties, 27–30,
        147–57
    rehearsal dinner, 40, 78–79, 157
Photographers, 42, 54, 73, 107–10
Pinterest, 130–32

Reception
    basics of, 101, 103
    costs of, 54, 71–72
    dancing at, 41, 259
    day of, 254–55
    drinks/beverages for, 54, 71,
        231–34
    food/catering for, 54, 71–72,
        103–5
    gifts at, 257, 260, 265
    last-minute details for, 260–61
    money-saving tips for, 231–34
    music for, 41–42, 73, 111–12
    nonprofit venues, 101, 238
    nontraditional reception,
        92–94
    order of events at, 257–60
    planning, 41–42, 80
    post-wedding reception, 67–68,
        158
    receiving line, 255–56
    toasts at, 261
    venue for, 71–72, 101–4
    welcome reception, 157
Rehearsal dinner
    costs of, 55
    etiquette for, 44–45

    invitations for, 45
    planning, 40, 78–79, 157
Religious officiants, 41, 54–55,
    72–73

Same-sex wedding, 196–200
San-san-kudo ceremony, 48
"Save the Date" cards, 44, 60, 139
Second wedding, 193–96, 206–8
Social media
    announcements on, 19–21
    guests and, 123–24
    privacy and, 19–21
    types of, 130–38
    for wedding planning, 120–40
Son-in-law, 33–39, 266–72. See also
    Groom
Stationery, 118–19

Timeline for wedding, 31, 272–75
Toasts, making, 53–54, 159, 261
Traditions, 42, 45–51, 119
Transportation, 54, 60–61, 101,
    115–16
Tumblr, 136–37
Twitter, 135–36

"Unplugged" wedding, 140

Vendors. See also specific vendors
    choosing, 13, 24, 103–15
    costs of, 54–55, 69, 71–73
    eco-friendly options for,
        98–101
    gratuities for, 71–73
    meeting with, 96–98, 144–45
    vendor meetings, 144–45
Videographers, 40, 54, 73, 107–8,
    110

Wedding. See also Wedding day
    budget for, 12–13, 25–26, 56–64

children at, 140, 195–96, 204,
216–17
civil ceremony, 102
cultural traditions for, 47–49
delicate situations at,
178–200
destination wedding, 64–67
eco-friendly options for,
98–101, 236–37
essentials for, 119
family members in, 41
music for, 73, 110–11
nonprofit venues, 101, 238
nontraditional ceremony,
92–93
nontraditional wedding,
92–95
planning, 30–31, 87–91,
95–119
post-ceremony events,
252–54
religious ceremony, 102
second wedding, 193–96
setting for, 101–2, 238
size of, 12, 24
timeline for, 31, 272–75
type of, 47–49, 92–93, 102
"unplugged" wedding, 140
Wedding apps, 120–23, 134,
138–40, 199
Wedding blogs, 124–25
Wedding cake, 105–7
Wedding day
arriving at ceremony, 249–51
hair appointments for, 244–45
last-minute details for, 260–61
makeup for, 245–46
overview of, 241–61
planning, 30–31, 87–91,
95–119
preparing for, 243–44
seating for, 41, 251

stress-free tips for, 242–43
vendors for, 246–48
Wedding dress
changing, 49
cost of, 54, 63, 100–101, 219
money-saving tips for, 100–
101, 227–31
previously worn dress, 100–
101, 229–31
renting, 230
selecting, 170–74
Wedding expenses, 52–73. See
also Expenses
Wedding planners, 32, 87–91
Wedding planning
with bride, 12, 21, 24
expectations of, 77–78
help with, 30–31, 87–91,
95–119
organization tips for, 30–32
rules of, 59
social media for, 120–40
timeline for, 31, 272–75
vendor meetings, 96–98
Welcome reception, 157